Paradise Island, heavenly journey

Jon Magee

authorHOUSE®

AuthorHouse™ UK Ltd.
500 Avebury Boulevard
Central Milton Keynes, MK9 2BE
www.authorhouse.co.uk
Phone: 08001974150

First published by AuthorHouse   11/15/2010

ISBN: 978-1-4520-4985-4 (sc)

This book is printed on acid-free paper.

In memory of Violet Magee (nee Hill) (1916 – 2009)
And her sister
Winifred Hill (1927 – 2005)

CONTENTS

ACKNOWLEDGEMENTS

There are many people that I would wish to express my appreciation to at the beginning of this book. It is a part of that desire that the book is dedicated to two ladies. Firstly, my mother, Violet Magee, who is central to this story and helped to provide so much detail which would not have been possible without her help. Secondly the book is dedicated to my aunt, my mother's sister, Winifred Hill. Winifred, or Aunt Winnie as we knew her, was a focal point of the wider family showing her warmth of character until she tragically died as a result of a mugging in her latter stage of life.

I must also acknowledge Dr. Kate Hartig who has given her time to read the manuscript and write the foreword. Kate comes with a wide knowledge of the Far East, including Singapore. It is particularly of note that she has given time to this during a year in which she was also working in Indonesia, beginning with the earthquake she lived through at the end of the year 2009.

FOREWORD BY DR KATE HARTIG

In his recently published first book *From Barren Rocks to Living Stones* Jon Magee recounts his teenage years living in Aden, Yemen, during the mid 1960s. In *Paradise Island* Jon travels back to an earlier period of his childhood. He reflects on his life as a young boy living with his family in Singapore during the 1950s. He discusses the trials and joy of British military family life living in what was once part of the British Empire. But like Jon's memoirs of Aden, the 1950s in Singapore was also a period of considerable change as Britain was forced to accept the ending of its colonial powers in far away 'exotic' places. But for Jon, it was an ideal childhood full of adventure and new experiences, from new foods to strange plants and significantly new friends that cut across cultural barriers.

Today, Singapore presents itself as a modern, bustling cosmopolitan city. With the kampongs (villages) and jungle areas now replaced by high- rise residential apartments and manicured parklands the perception of Singapore as a "paradise island" is possibly difficult to comprehend. But Jon's memories brings back an earlier time when life was perhaps not so much simpler but different. So different that it was life changing. This story is set within the context of many journeys, Jon's journey through early childhood, the family's journeys between Singapore and Britain and most significantly his parents' profound spiritual journey back to their saviour and God.

Dr Kate Hartig (PhD)

INTRODUCTION

My previous book, *"From barren rocks ... to living stones"*, majored upon my experiences regarding the events in Aden in nineteen sixty six and nineteen sixty seven during the terrorism of the time and the major British evacuation in nineteen sixty seven. These were major historical land marks, but it was the people who made the story so real. *"Paradise Island, heavenly journey"* looks back to the experiences in the Far East in the nineteen fifties. I was far younger, but history was still the issue, surrounded by people who had adult concerns following the Second World War. It is the stories of the people that will be found within this book.

"Paradise Island, heavenly journey" seeks to draw out some of those personal stories that puts the meat into the years lived out in the world, the real history that exceeds the isolation of politics on their own. Someone rightly said that no man is an island. We see the wealth of our personal stories as we see how we interact with each other, and as the stories of those we have walked the journey of life with reveal how we each have some influence upon each other. We have a story to tell because the story of another has guided us onto a new milestone of life. This book speaks of my early life and the family I grew up with, but it also will draw on the stories of those who touched our lives as individuals and also as a family.

During my own schooling, history meant nothing to me for many years. It was merely a dry catalogue of dates and statistics that seemed, to me, to be so boring. That was to change with the arrival of a new teacher to the school. He brought a new approach to the class room which opened my eyes to the present day relevance of all that was taught. His excitement as he spoke of the story was evident, and it was as if he lived out every detail of the story for himself, a real person at the centre of the events. At that moment, there was a new dimension that had arrived on the horizon for me. Immediately the realisation was there, this was about real people, just as today must be looked back on by our descendents recognising our lives and aspirations as people must always be paramount to their study. This is the heart of the excitement that can be ours today as we reflect upon the past.

There is, however, not just the interacting of humanity with humanity. The story of our life makes even more sense when it is revealed in its holistic fullness, with the various aspects of our life being drawn together as one, each supporting and enhancing the other. Even within the secular world, there are those who will acknowledge that we have lives made up of the emotional, the physical, and also the spiritual. As well as the interacting of humanity, this book reveals the interacting also in this way. Wherever the reader may stand on this issue, may I give the assurance that at the heart of this book is the story of real people, real events, and real lives, all lived out in the international world, each playing a part in their sphere of history.

CHAPTER 1

"Move it?"

Jon scrambled across the rocks, clambering as quickly as he could manage, under the scorching heat that was very much accepted as being the normal climatic conditions of Aden, in the southern Arabian Peninsula, whilst still seeking to ensure he had a safe foothold as each step was placed in front of the other. The whole exercise was far from easy when one bears in mind that the rocks that he was negotiating were often reaching an unbearable temperature as they reflected the high atmospheric temperatures in the surrounding area that would rarely be less than one hundred degrees Fahrenheit, with very little rainfall. What Aden lacked in rainfall it exuded in heat and sunshine.

Most countries experience four seasons in the course of a year, there would be spring, summer, autumn and winter. Aden had just the two, the one that was known as "the hot season" and on the other extreme there was what was known as "the even hotter season." Winter had no apparent place in the life of the residents of Aden. Weather forecasts were quite a boring occupation, with such predictability as to what each day would bring. There was such a contradiction here to the British preoccupation in which a conversation opener must always

1

revolve around the changing weather. The very question about what the day was going to bring would always be a non starter in this part of the world.

As the day would progress, the temperature of the rocks would appear to become even greater, retaining the heat that was already there whilst adding to it with the accumulation of the beating of the sun that developed each hour since the sun had risen first thing in the morning. Perhaps it would be partly for that reason that there would be an added leap and a spring in his step as he made his way across from one position to another sensing the heat beneath his bare feet that would sting at each step he would take.

He could well imagine the feelings of those who performed the eastern tricks of walking across the burning coals, just as each rock would hold the heat all day for all who ventured to walk upon them with their bare feet. It was an extremely difficult climb that involved using the hands as well as the feet but no ropes, but it was always seen to be worthwhile to gain an opportunity to spend time escaping from the realities of Aden life, with all of its senseless violence and fanatical terrorism that was so prevalent in the nineteen sixties.

This, for him, was a wonderful haven from everything, basking within the peacefulness of it all as he anchored himself into his chosen place of shelter. Before him was a panoramic vision that was beyond compare. Jon appreciated those times when the violence of Aden life in the nineteen sixties was safely forgotten, at least for a short time. The view itself was sufficiently rewarding enough to justify the time that had been taken or the effort that had been made. Sitting from the vantage point of the great height of the rocks above, he could manage to look around in each and every direction that surrounded him and survey the view, soaking in the wonder of it all, this was truly something that was quite amazing.

Looking beyond the sandy beach, where some of his

family and friends would be sunbathing and relaxing, or even swimming for those who were feeling a bit more energetic, and then looking on across the bay with its wonderful hue of blue and green water. This was an exceedingly pleasant sight to see the water, uncluttered with the contamination that would usually be seen in much of the Western waters where he had come from, here was a sea that was clear and sparkling with the reflection of the sun. Then ultimately came the opportunity to be able to look out beyond the bay and on into the Aden Gulf.

Within these waters was encompassed so much that symbolised the very essence of life. The gulf's marine life, indeed, was extremely rich in both the quantity and also the variety of its species. The seasonally variable up welling of waters in the coastal zone provided the surface layer of water with a considerable supply of nutrient elements, which also produced an abundant growth of plankton. Sardines and mackerel abounded in these areas. The main type of open sea fish would have to be the dolphin, though technically Dolphins are really mammals living in the sea, not fish. They have always had a universal appeal when seen, each of them symbolizing the combined experiences of freedom, joy, grace and serenity, uplifting the spirits of many people all around the world.

In addition there were plenty of the fast swimming tuna, billfish, and also the meat eating sharks, which are known to have the most powerful jaws in the world. Some people had even spoken of seeing the odd whale when out at sea. In the midst of the ocean they could observe these large, magnificent, intelligent, aquatic mammals with their sleek, streamlined bodies that can move easily through the water. The first sign that whales were around was usually the blow as it would breathe through the blow hole on the top of its head. When it expelled its breath, the resulting burst of air and water vapour could be seen as far away as two kilometres on a clear day. The gulf also provided a breeding ground for sea turtles, and rock lobsters were abundant as well. Life was bursting forth in all directions.

Yet Jon could also see the shipping going past. This was the main shipping route that lay between the Far East and the United Kingdom, and as such from here one could view the transportation of the world coming in and going out, but for him, it was also a very significant major link to recalling aspects of Jon's past, as well as his family, and the life they had all lived during the nineteen fifties. It was the musician, Acker Bilk, who recorded the instrumental music of his record, "Stranger on the shore", in nineteen sixty two, but as Jon was looking out to sea he did not feel like a stranger on any shore, because he felt in some strange way as if he was at this moment identifying with a whole world that was full of people that came from every race and nation, and from every continent that could be imagined.

Within his imagination, it was no longer a matter of reaching out into the world, for the world had now been instantaneously drawn to him in the most unique experience possible. Identification with people has to mean something far more than just another scene in life. There was a tremendous beauty to be appreciated as all the colours of the world united into a rainbow of people, every race blended as one. It was the sixteenth Century John Donne that once said, "No man is an island". He was declaring that no one should be seen in isolation of each other, but that mankind must be seen as being interconnected with each other, every man is a piece of a wider continent, a part of the main body of land.

It was at this point that Jon could feel that he was identifying not so much with a world that was divided by water, but rather it was like a "bridge over troubled waters", as the singers Simon and Garfunkel would have expressed it in the song they sung that came with those words of the same title. Rather than seeing the water as something that spoke of division between the nations of the world, here was the one thing that was drawing together the various fragments of existence, and unifying them into one story of life.

Here was a connection that seemed to tie everything

together. There were just the four members of the family that were living in Aden, his dad, Paddy, who was serving with the British Royal Air Force, his mother, Violet, and his sister who preferred these days to be known by an abbreviation of her middle name, Pat, and himself, of course. Prior to living in Aden Pat would have been known by her first name, Geraldine. Likewise, in the nineteen fifties, Jon would also have responded to a different name, as his birth certificate would have recorded the longer name of Jonathan. Now, like his sister, he was quite happy to use an abbreviation of the name as he was called Jon. Perhaps that was part of the aspects of stamping one's own seal upon the essential identity of one's self as young people grow up through those periods of adolescence and in the process develop their own unique character and personality.

There were also four older children in the family who had now reached an age to become independent and leave the family home, but would nevertheless have been a part of the international voyages of the nineteen fifties. Margot was the eldest in the family, followed by the twins, David and Kathleen, and then there was Dennis, in all there were eleven years difference in the ages between the eldest and the youngest of the six children. Together they had travelled the world and been at the centre of some of the most sensitive moments in political history. Sometimes that would mean taking a risk, and stepping away from the security of life that was lived in the shallow end of the pool of living, but the benefits come with such risks. As George Eliot had expressed it, "I would not creep along the coast, but steer out in mid sea, by guidance of the stars." Going out on a limb can be very scary in life but that's where the best fruit is growing, waiting for us to grasp and claim it for ourselves.

The family had collectively known a wealth of adventures and experiences that most young people of their ages would rarely have had any insight into. The triviality of tourism was not to be their means of voyaging. Travelling was indeed to be the experience that was to be the hub of life for them and everything else was meant to revolve around that central hub. In many senses, of course, it was rightly considered to be a very privileged life; to be born and to grow up as the child of a serviceman must be recognised as giving one a unique background and upbringing. They discovered between them the fullness of the world's riches in terms of natural experiences that were spread throughout the world. True wealth does not need to be measured in the currency of nations, but in the global currency that is discovered in the relating to the people of the world of various cultures. Travelling the world is, of course, an eye opening education in itself in so many different and wonderful ways.

In the days that preceded when there was more regular air travel that was operating, the British Armed Forces travelled by sea to all the corners of the world and this would have continued to be the practice up to and including the nineteen fifties. The Ministry of Transport gave contracts with civilian shipping lines to build and manage troopships and often they would be prepared to make a certain amount of financial contributions to ensure their construction was completed satisfactorily. As Jon looked out across the sea, he was still a mere teenager with a future ahead, but these connections with sea travellers passing by revived the memories of a childhood that had been lived out in the past even further east in Singapore.

Seeing those ships that were passing by in those waters was seen as being a clear and vivid reminder of the last time he would have also passed that way by ship, along with his family, less than a decade before, late in the year of nineteen fifty eight. Jonathan, as we shall refer to him now within these pages, was the youngest of those six children in the family. They had boarded the troop ship, Empire Fowey, in Singapore on route for Southampton on the south coast of England, and recalled passing this very piece of coastland. The ship was a labyrinth of companionways leading to decks on which were cabins, troop accommodation, crew quarters and such functional areas as ablutions, administration offices, recreation saloons, store rooms and messing. As he looked out to sea in this moment in time, so he envisaged the passengers would also no doubt have looked back as he would have done all those years before. The view on that juncture in time, however, would clearly have been different to the vision he had on this occasion, as they looked from an opposing direction, out from the sea towards the barren Aden coastline.

In the distance, the passengers on board the ship would have seen a line of crags that were rising up out of the water, these each resolved themselves into sharp saw backed ridges of rock, cliffs and peaked mountains which were brown in colour and streaked with reds and blacks as they approached. Then there would be the startling realisation that this was not just any huge rock that was butting out of the sea; in fact this was their first sight of Aden. There was not one little tree to be seen as they looked out! There was not one blade of grass that was visible! There was not one patch of vegetation or vivid green of plant to be surveyed! There was absolutely no indication of life being displayed upon the land. In every direction, the view seemed to be much the same. Words could never possibly fully convey the impression of the extreme aridity and desolation of Aden, a community of people that were fixed among a series of extinct volcanoes.

Then, in all of its forbidding majesty of desolated beauty, Shamsan, the mountain peak that towered above the Gulf of Aden, looked down upon the whole length and breadth of the country with such an extreme magnificence, and splendour, and dignity. It was truly an impressive vision that came in its own right, completely overshadowing everything else in view capturing the eyes of all who surveyed the scene. Great huge bare mountains, rocks and buildings were all that seemed to be available for them to be seen, the hot sun pouring down in full strength.

Who would have thought that just a few years later, at least for some of the family, it was to be this same land that would be destined to become their home! This was beyond the wildest imagination of any one of them. But for now, as they looked on across the bay, this location could only be perceived as being just a transitory visit as the family was currently destined for far more distant places on their voyage of life. There was a far wider world that was beckoning them, and demanding their immediate attention. How could there be anything permanent or lasting about these sights before them, because as they floated across the seas of time this could never be understood as being anything more than existing only for a relatively short period of time. Yet clearly such a place of residence was destined to be an integral part of their future.

The Empire Fowey, itself, had come to develop an extremely interesting and colourful history which could easily arouse the attention of any observers as being something that was full of such variety, challenge and excitement. The ship, however, had been initially built under the name of the "Potsdam" in nineteen thirty six for the Far East service of the North German Lloyd, but during the period of the Second World War it was used as a troop and accommodation ship. Throughout the duration of the war she was to see service in so many differing places, and to experience so much within the conflicts, for the "sake of the Fatherland", Germany. As the war was coming to its completion, perhaps there would be some of the crew who would have had high hopes and dreams and aspirations of returning to a more civilian function, perhaps still serving in the same ship within that role, but it was not going to be the case for them. These idealistic desires and ambitions were going to be found just outside their reach.

She was commandeered by the British Royal Navy in May

nineteen forty five at Flensburg, and was then renamed as the Empire Fowey, and used then as a British troopship under the Pacific and Orient, or the more familiar title of "P and O", management. In the days before air travel was to become so extensively and regularly used, the British Armed Forces travelled by sea to all the corners of the world. Often the Troop ship, Empire Fowey, would be commissioned to travel between the island of Singapore in the Far East and Southampton in the south of England. Southampton was one of the UK's busiest ports, and a principal driver in the regional economy and was the main gateway for Far East imports.

Following the occasion of a fire breaking out on board in nineteen sixty, whilst berthed at Southampton, she was then sold to the Pan-Islamic Shipping Company of Pakistan where she was assigned to be used on a pilgrim service to Jeddah, which was the main gate through which most of the pilgrims arrived by air and sea, or the Islamic holy city of Mecca, until she was eventually destined to be decommissioned and broken up in nineteen seventy six. In this new pilgrim role, she would regularly have continued to travel past Aden, just as she did in her previous life, as she fulfilled her new function of conveying the religious travellers on their pilgrimage around the world. For those who would take the time to observe and to spy her out from the distance she was regularly taking her place amongst the armada of vessels passing by heading for the Red Sea. It was surely a very varied and diverse shipping experience that had been known by the Empire Fowey and its crew, one that was so full of the depth of drama and excitement.

However, whatever the circumstances may have been for the ship, it could never compare with the drama that went with a mother that was travelling the world with a family of six young children. The family's life in some respects could so easily reflect the lyrics of the popular song of the day, "I've been everywhere man, never worry or care man, I've been everywhere." Children are known to be often naturally looking for that sense of adventure, seeking to capture the excitement of life, whatever the risks may be, never fully realizing, or understanding, the extent of the dangers that would engulf them as they look to themselves as being invincible whatever may be the scrapes they may end up in along the way. They were sure that they were incapable of being defeated in any of the events of life they would meet, living as if they were "Supermen" even if they were more likely to have had a greater resemblance in every way to that mild mannered man who was known to the surrounding world as Clark Kent.

Violet, as the mother, would know differently of course as she sought to guide and to protect each one of her young children, even when it came down to literally grabbing one of the children by the ankles as they sought to enquire at a closer range the wonder of the sea life that surrounded them on their journey, in his curiosity he just wished to be able to find out a little bit more about the things that had now become an integral part of his daily environment, as he leaned far too far for his own safety over the edge of the ship's deck. It was a Jewish proverb that said "God could not be everywhere and therefore he made mothers." In such situations, one realises how wise those words are, and how important is the role of the mother in many families.

"EMPIRE FOWEY"

There is an old saying which says that "Curiosity killed the cat, but satisfaction cured it." Most of us remember the first part of the saying but it is only by looking at it in the context of the fuller statement that we come to understand the meaning of the saying at its best. The young boy perhaps was thinking that his complete satisfaction would be achieved only once he had found the answers to all his questioning of the strange life at sea. Perhaps it was a childish notion on his part, that something as beautiful and enticing as the deep blue sea that was surrounding them would never hurt or cause him harm, but with the experience of life one soon learns differently. Reality is often born in the midst of maturity.

If the husbands were ever on board the same ship as the families, which would not always be the case, then they would be accommodated in a different part of the ship away from the women and children in a dormitory style room that was filled with row after row of three tiered bunk beds. Violet, therefore, would have had the completely exclusive responsibility for all of the children as they crossed the oceans of the world. Upon her shoulders there would be required the full parental decisions, knowing that unique mix of tender loving care that was blended together with firm authority. Often she needed to mix those roles of mother and father to ensure the children had the essential input as they developed and grew within such an unnatural environment. That ability to mix those characteristics together was a quality that was so essential for the young family to survive the demands that come with the tough and arduous life of sea travel, with all of the harshness and difficulties that are an integral part of such an experience of the nomadic life they had come to be accustomed to.

There were the times that would come with a touch of comedy as they took each voyage that lay before them. There would always be the lasting memory of a young boy, who was sitting so very "innocently" beside a gate on the deck of the ship. Passersby would be heard to "coo" and "aah" and tell mum what a well behaved boy he was. Violet would feel an inner sense of pride as she then began to move on with her son, only to hear a loud crash coming from behind them, followed by the even louder commotion of the seaman shouting and cursing as the very same heavy metal gate had inexplicably fallen upon his feet. It was no wonder that he shouted so loudly about the incompetence of whoever had foolishly left the gate in such a dangerous condition, the great weight of the metal falling upon his feet would have created an incredible pain. No one could understand how that could have possibly have happened. However, there was a sense of extreme relief that was felt by all that the young well behaved child, who had been sitting there at risk just moments before, had been moved away from the scene before the disaster had struck.

It was only later at the end of that day, however, that Violet would come to understand how the accident had been caused; though she was equally determined that she would not say a word to any other person. It was to be her personal secret that must never be revealed to the wider world. As she began to empty the pockets of the young boy's clothes that evening prior to putting them into the laundry, she was to find an amazing pocket full of various nuts and bolts. The contents of a small boys pocket tell many a story, it has been said. Many mothers may have had the same kind of experience when emptying the pockets of a young boy, but ironically these ones were just like the ones that had once been fitted on the ships gate holding everything together. The similarity to them appeared to be more than a mere coincidence. Could it be possible that the boy who had given the impression that he had been "innocently" sitting beside the ships gate knew considerably more about the cause of the disaster that had occurred than he had previously been admitting to? Had his in built sense of curiosity created more to the story of the accident than had previously been realized? When questioned about it he was reported to have said that he was curious as to how everything worked together.

There would be the occasions of anxiety and apprehension, fear and worry. Life boat and fire drill on each of the ships would happen to them so frequently that one might be forgiven for wondering and speculating as to whether the crew already knew of some impending shipping tragedy that was threatening to happen to them on the journey. Life boat drills for all passengers were a compulsory requirement. For most passengers, this was inevitably the least exciting part of the voyage they were undertaking. But, they were assured, it was always important for the well being of all the passengers and crew and it would not take long for the drill to be completed.

The passengers were not so sure about that, sensing that the monotonous routine would take far longer than they desired despite the reassurances that were given to them. The passengers had to know in detail which route they would need to take in the event of any emergency occurring, where the assembly points were located, how they were to don a life jacket, and where each of the life boats were situated. Somewhere in the cabin would be a diagram of the ship with little arrows pointing out the route that would need to be taken from the cabin to the "assigned" life boat station. It was imperative that the details of this map were committed to memory. The whole exercise of working through this procedure was a chore, a task that was seen to be far from enjoyable by the passengers of all ages, and one that was such a waste of time, one might think, but in the midst of the ocean, such detailed knowledge could literally mean the difference between life and death.

One dark night, the terrifying reality of it all was to finally sink home deeply and most profoundly for them in a manner that was never going to be forgotten in the years that would lie ahead. All the rehearsing and practicing they had been experiencing was about to be played out for real with such an intensity that it was inevitable that they would begin to fully live out each aspect of the life boat drill. There could never be room left for any vagueness of knowledge when you know this is for real. Living the experience was to become the fulfillment of all the educating drill. No longer did one think that all the practices and life boat drills were a waste of time. It was essential for life, and without it the luxury of time would cease to exist for them all.

The children were all safely tucked into their beds for the night. Peace and quiet for mother had arrived at last! Serenity, silence, and calmness, finally it was the haven of the day. Violet checked the children out just one more time just to reassure her that everything was completely well. Yes, they were sleeping, with the exception of the eldest, Margot. It was at this time of the night that Violet had the chance to make use of the bath room, which lay down the corridor, without any disturbance. Margot was left with the responsibility of ensuring that each of the younger children were kept safe and accounted for, as Violet made her way down the corridor armed with a bath towel and wash kit and toiletries. The bath water was run; the opportunity she had been waiting for had finally arrived.

It was at that crucial moment that the dreaded disaster was going to strike the ship; the alarm was sounded through the whole ship by the tannoy system. There was a fire on board! This was not merely a practice, came the repeated message, this was for real! The thought sprung through the mind, what an inconsiderate timing, but the reality is that disasters will often spring forth at the most inconsiderate of times, at a time when it was least expected.

Despite that, this was something that had to be taken seriously by them all. Of all the disasters which can befall a vessel at sea, fire is considered to be the most devastating. Marine fire incidents are very dangerous and very destructive and historically have been responsible for the loss of a considerable number of lives. Ship fires are second only to shipwrecks when it comes to calculating the number of casualties and total loss of life.

The crisis they had been preparing for so often during each of the fire drills had finally arrived, and therefore the appropriate response from them all was vital. Their ultimate survival would be depending upon it.

It was soon after the alarm had been sounded that there was a loud knock at the door, as Margot desperately called out, "Mum, there's a fire on board! What will we do?" Calmly, Violet responded giving her instructions and trying to bring some reassurance. Simultaneously she sought to find her own clothing, "Waken the rest of the children quickly," she said, "do not wait for me, but make sure that you all make your way together onto the deck. Just remember the drill you have been through and the instructions you have heard so many times before. I will be right behind you, do not worry, everything will be alright."

Violet would have wanted to be with her children, but she realized that for their safety it was equally imperative that she allowed someone else to accept the delegation of responsibility, rather than them waiting till she was ready. She could hear people moving out from their cabins, and then heading along the corridor towards the lifeboat deck. As they passed by, Violet could visualise the routine that they were all going through, having attended so many life boat drills during her various voyages. She had been there so many times that she could have gone through the motions even in her sleep. As the passengers and crew assembled underneath the lifeboats, one group to the port side and another group to the starboard, their names would be called out from the official passenger list. The deck officer in charge of each lifeboat verified the names to make sure that nobody was missing.

Meanwhile, Violet continued to ensure she was completely respectable and then made her way along the empty corridors and up onto the deck and began her desperate search for the children. Like many mothers who had gone before her, the safety of her children was always the first priority in every eventuality. She appeared to be the last passenger to make their way along that deserted corridor to safety. Panic seemed to be the order of the day as she arrived on the deck as many people appeared out of control in the midst of fear and distress, and some of them were seen to have dashed hurriedly on deck in all manner of state of dress, with some merely wearing a towel that was wrapped loosely around them! Not everyone had followed Violet's example of calmly taking the time to ensure that they were suitably dressed for the occasion. The fear of the unknown can often bring some interesting reactions from humanity.

Smoke was billowing from the solitary funnel that was towering above, though that may seem fairly normal. This time, however, there was more than the normal as a result of the fire which had started in that area, however seeing it in these circumstances seemed to emphasize the drama of the whole situation. Violet knew where they had all been instructed to gather, and so her first thoughts that night were that she should make her way to the pre-arranged spot as soon as she could, armed with the life jackets ready to put onto each one of the children. As a hen would have gathered her chicks protectively as close to her as possible in times of disaster, so was her desire.

As she looked at each of them, she began to be filled with alarm with the discovery she made. One of the children was missing! Even with six children, a mother soon knows that one of her own is missing. There was no doubt in her mind, she had looked at each one of them in turn and only five faces could be seen returning her concerned looks. She called across to Margot, "Where is everyone? Where is your brother? I cannot see him anywhere!" He was missing!

Margot had woken him, along with all the others, and ensured that they were all ready and told them to all follow closely as they made their way to the designated Assembly Point. She had fulfilled that responsibility perfectly. Yet somewhere in the midst of all the swell of passengers that were desperately seeking to find the way to safety, the young boy had not managed to reach the intended destination. He was lost, in a ship that was destined to become a ship wreck resting on the bed of the ocean, a home for the fishing creatures of the sea. The prospect of it all was more than any mother could feel comfortable taking into consideration.

There was no alternative for Violet. She knew exactly what she needed to do, and there was no time available for hesitation or for the luxury of debating the wisdom of it all. Timing was of the essence, the saving of a young boy's life depended on it. She was a mother, and any mother would no doubt have reacted in much the same way when realizing that she had a child that was in danger. The first hurdle, however, was to find a way of getting past the crew that was guarding the doorway back into the heart of the ailing ship. No one was permitted to return in that direction. Violet was small in stature, some four foot ten inches, and slightly built, but not one member of the crew were big enough to prevent her going through, no matter how huge they may have been in terms of physical stature. She was small, but the words vertically challenged did not seem to be appropriate as she challenged the seamen that lay before her. They were a human barrier between her and the child she was missing, but in this moment in time she was determined they would not remain as a barrier, they were merely hurdles that were placed there for her to overcome.

Physical stature is not everything when confronted with such a desperate situation as this. The crew explained to her that there will soon come a time when the door will be shut. The whole area she was seeking to reach would be completely sealed off. No one will be able to move such heavy doors which are designed to keep any flood water contained to one part of the ship, as well as acting as a break against the spread of any fires that may possibly develop. If that happens whilst she is situated on the wrong side of the doors then there is little hope for her survival.

They may have sought to reason with her as much as they could, but Violet was not prepared to submit to their perception of logic. Defiantly she declared, "I do not care about that, what does matter above everything else is that my son has no hope at all of survival if I do not make an attempt to return and find him before the door is finally closed! Can you imagine a young child standing on the other side of that door you are speaking of? I am going and there is nothing or anyone who will be able stop me", she said with a renewed sense of determination. They saw the look in her face, and knew she definitely meant business as she brushed past them and sped on her way without looking back. A mother's love will always put everything into a different perspective. George Bernard Shaw once said, "*Some men see things as they are and ask why. Others dream things that never were and ask why not.*" Such is the spirit that drives some forward to achieve what others will idly call the impossible never daring to attempt. Violet still had the dream in her heart of a child returned to her arms.

Violet hurried down as fast as she could. She knew that time was crucial if her mission was ever to prove to be successful in anyway, and it was crucial that she did succeed. As she made her way along Violet looked into every conceivable hiding place, anywhere imaginable that a young boy could have concealed himself away in. Any door that may have been left even slightly ajar, any entrance way, was open territory for her to investigate.

There was not even the slightest sighting of him upon the way. When she reached the cabin she was becoming desperate. He was supposed to have followed the rest of the family down the corridor; surely he could not be here at the start of the journey. Yet every other possibility had been covered, what was there to lose, she thought, as she pushed the door fully open.

Her eyes opened wide in disbelieve as she came through the doorway, for there he was, the boy of the moment, fast asleep in his bunk bed! The one who had caused every one such despair and anxiety lay sleeping as if there was not a reason in the world to have any concern about him. His face gave the appearance of a picture of angelic innocence.

He had certainly been woken from his slumbers, and prepared with everyone else. Each one of the children had passed through the door to begin the exodus from the cabin in order to join with the other passengers. However, in the midst of his drowsy composure, he had assumed he had been woken to visit the toilet, as many young children might be in the midst of the night. He had made his way through and completed the task he had wrongly assumed had been set for him, and then returned sleepily to his bunk bed, without giving a thought as to why no one else was present in the room any more.

Somehow, his shoes were missing, but he was there, which was far more important than any materialistic concerns. Even now, it may be too late for them both, but it was important for her to give priority to attempting to rejoin the rest of the family, as well as the passengers and crew assembled on the deck. However, now there was a weight that had been lifted off her shoulders even if she was carrying the young boy. Now there was some joy that had replaced the anxiety, there was a spring in her step, even if there was still a mammoth task to complete as she raced against time. Time was something there was too little available to them.

She turned the corner, and her heart leapt for joy as she saw a chink of light ahead where the heavy metal door was situated, a chink of light that sent the message that the completion of the mission was imminent. However, the hopes that had swelled up inside her were very nearly dashed at that last moment. It was just at that point that the crew received the orders, "Close the doors!" As they prepared to do so, putting their full weight behind the door, one of them casually looked around the edge of the door. "Wait!" he called, "there is someone coming, a woman and a child!" Saved just in the nick of time! The family gathered together for their reunion, reassured that they were now once again complete as a family ought to be. It seemed like an age that they had all waited as the life boats were attended to, being prepared for the important launch they would all be dependent on. Then they were to hear the "all clear". The fire had been extinguished; it was safe to return to normal. For at least one family on board, however, normal would now take on a completely new meaning.

Then there would be the concerns of schooling. As Nelson Mandela expressed it so eloquently, "Education is the most powerful weapon with which to change the world". If the young people were to have any part in the changing world ahead this was an important aspect to address as they voyaged across the world. Travel should be an education in itself, what is learned from such experiences would help influence and mould the lives of the children in the years that lay ahead. However, there still needs to be some consideration given to the formal aspect that may be discovered from a schools perspective. The journey from the Far East to Southampton, in England, by sea would take so long, arrangements needed to be taken to account for the educational needs of each of the children.

The dining room was large enough to accommodate everyone for meals. Once the meals were completed, the dining room was then converted instantaneously into a mobile school. Each class had its own area set apart. Open plan schooling has its disadvantages, not least being the ease with which the children can easily be distracted by the neighbouring class. Every sound could be heard, yet at the same time this would be the best one could do to ensure that some form of learning could continue, irrespective as to whether the facilities were adequate enough.

Then there was the opportunity of the traditional "school

trip", to see the ships bridge. Within the confines of the ship, that was about as far as one could go as the details of sailing the seven seas were explained in practical detail. With an officer and sailor, and often the captain, on watch, they were always able to learn something. The chart and navigation room was open to everyone, as were places to view the equipment and instruments. The bridge was a fascinating part of the ship and often a great place for seeing even further into the horizon and thereby providing a great view!

In small groups, the children were shown all that lay behind the average working day of the crew, imagining they were the ship's captain with the full responsibility of guiding the ship into each and every port having charted the oceans of the world on the journey, and seeing the charts that detailed where the ship was and where it had been. Seen through the eyes of the young, this was a magical moment that they were able to cherish.

There was also the education of the sea. Not merely water, but the life that would fill it and encompass it. To be able to look out from the deck and to see sights that could never have been imagined from the text book of a land blocked school was something that would fill many a young child with awe, allowing ones imagination to stretch to tremendous lengths. It was an unbelievable sight for Jonathan as he looked out and saw for the first time a school of flying fish. Of course, the flying fish did not fly, in the sense of flapping its wing sized fins, but it did actually glide. The fish would build up its speed underwater, swimming toward the surface with its fins folded tightly against its streamlined body. Upon breaking the surface, the fish would then spread its enlarged fins and gain additional thrust from rapid beats of the still submerged tail. When sufficient speed had been attained, the tail was lifted clear of the water and the fish was then airborne, gliding a few feet above the surface at a speed of about sixteen Kilometres per hour, or ten miles per hour, performing feats one would have considered impossible for the average fish.

The fish were also capable of making several consecutive glides, the tail propelling it up again and again each time it would sink back down to the surface. The stronger fliers could span as much as one hundred and eighty metres, or six hundred feet, in one single glide, and compound glides, timed as long as forty seconds, may cover four hundred metres, or thirteen hundred feet. The flying fish could be found in any one of the major oceans of the world, but mainly in the warm tropical and subtropical waters of the Atlantic, Pacific, and Indian oceans. Flight for these fishes was primarily considered a means of escaping from any stalking predators that may have been seeking to defeat them in the water, but not purely for that reason alone. Flying fish can manage to attain sufficient height to carry them even onto the decks of any ships that would be voyaging in the midst of their waters, where their remains have frequently been discovered by the seamen at dawn.

As Jonathan looked out for the first time he was filled with a complete and utter amazement as the fish would appear to be leaping in all kinds of directions. He was even more amazed to hear that they were referred to as being a school of fish and with that concept began to think of how important schooling must be throughout the whole of creation, and not just humanity, as he imagined the fish endeavouring to leap up to see their class blackboard. Clearly he had not grasped the different ways in which the word school could be used, but he had certainly experienced an education for himself that day that was well beyond measure.

Another place where the sea life has much to reveal is the Bay of Biscay. The Bay of Biscay is a gulf off the North Atlantic Ocean. It lies along the western coast of France from Brest south to the Spanish border, and the northern coast of Spain, and is named for the Spanish province of Biscay. The bay is literally alive, with fish, with whales and dolphins, with birds and even insects! For those with an interest in such things, it is a paradise full of the wonder of creation. Yet it is not the natural wild life that would be a fixed memory for the family.

The bay is also noted for its sudden, severe storms and its strong currents that would be daunting for the most seasoned of sea travellers. The surface currents of the Bay of Biscay are influenced by the clockwise circulation in the North Atlantic that produced a clockwise circulation in the bay. The Bay of Biscay is noted among sailors for its extremely rough seas, and such is its severity that it has become known to some as being the valley of death. It was a passage of water that was surely to be feared by all. Gales can be very severe and may be known to exceed seventy miles, or one hundred and thirteen kilometres, per hour. Squalls are also a hazard to navigation and may occur at any time of the year. And it was the storms that were to become the most lasting memory for the family when they came to face the Bay of Biscay.

Green faces, objects flying through the air all night long, walls, floors, and mattresses creaking and groaning as the ship lurched yet again in different directions. Then there were the stomachs that were experiencing zero gravity for the nth time. It wasn't fun for anyone by any manner of imagination, as one seeks to find a means of bearing the effects or else just waiting on the body's natural response to three arduous days on an extreme roller coaster ride. To think that there could be people who would pay for even ten minutes of this kind of turbulent experience on the fairground! One moment one would be looking down into the foreboding depth of the sea, the next it seemed one was looking up into the angry looking sky, and then it was into the fearsome sea again. Few would escape the demoralising feelings of sea sickness as they passed through the bay.

It was extremely hard to be excited about anything within these circumstances except surviving another night, or day, without throwing up. One poor fellow was reportedly left in his cabin with just his pills and a stick of rock for two days! No one wanted to stomach anything; they just wanted it to end. And eventually it did! In general, the centrally located cabins experienced the least amount of motion and were always preferable in these situations; though there was no guarantee of getting ones preferred cabin. Certainly, if there were port holes in the cabin it was essential to ensure that these were all closed. Failure to exercise such caution has left many a poor person awash with the contents of the sea, which is far from an ideal situation from anyone's perspective.

Then again, there would be the day to day domestic issues to contend with as the family travelled the world. As the family settled into the cabin one evening, each with their chosen bunk beds they had selected, one of the children was to get a sudden and very unpleasant awakening. Nobody was really sure how it could have happened, whether the ship had lurched in a new direction, or just that the child had naturally turned in his sleep. All they knew was that he had fallen from the top bunk bed onto the floor below. Being on the top bunk bed can often be an attraction to young children in any family as it added to the sense of adventure and excitement on the voyage, but equally it can also increase the risks in times of accidents. It does not take a lot of "rocket science" knowledge to be aware that there will be greater chances of injury sustained from a fall that is experienced from a greater height.

They were somewhere in the midway position of the Indian Ocean at the time, which was a body of water that is covering approximately one fifth of the total ocean area of the earth, and constituted the third largest ocean. It stretched between Africa on the West and Australia, Java, and Sumatra on the East, which separated in the North into the Arabian Sea and the Bay of Bengal; the monsoons, or trade winds, blew here with great regularity; from April to October they were strong from the South West, and from October to April they were more gentle coming in the opposite direction.

However, the most important information for the family to contend with was that a young child had not only fallen from his bunk bed, but was also lying motionless on the cabin floor. They tried hard to encourage him to get up, but on each occasion he declared he was unable to move. One member of the family was sent running to get help from the sick bay, but was only able to get as far as the Purser who immediately took control of the situation. It was clear that the child had struck his head hard as he fell to the floor.

All head injuries are potentially serious and require proper assessment because they can result in impaired consciousness. Indeed, there are occasions where what may have appeared to be a minor head injury can cause enough damage to later lead to becoming a fatality. A head injury can lead to a small tear of an artery, causing blood to leak into the space between the skull itself and the brain, forming a growing clot. The patient may not feel anything at first, but inside their skull the blood clot is rapidly getting bigger, and the situation soon becomes critical. Within the expanse of the ocean there is little that one can do to address the dangers.

That undetected small bleeding between the brain and skull was like a time bomb waiting to explode with the potential of change within a matter of days as the appearance of one full of life can lead to one that is facing imminent death through the experience of a traumatic brain injury. There was no other option to take at that moment as the child was lifted up and gently carried to the sick bay where he was placed under medical observation by the doctors and nurses who were on duty until they reached the Port of Aden.

One of the oldest buildings in Aden was the Royal Air Force Hospital, perched high on the hill above Steamer Point and Tawahi. This one hundred and eighty bed hospital served all of the British Forces in the Aden Protectorate, and their families, and also any passing merchant seamen in the area of all nationalities. This building was to be the greatest hope of medical assistance for this young boy at sea. The hospital would have the access of so much support and appropriate equipment to ensure any relevant tests were carried out.

It was imperative that he was given more specialised attention than could ever be realised on board ship, not knowing whether he may have gained a fractured skull through the incident. For some people, this would have seemed like the highlight of the voyage, as the crowd gathered around to watch as if this was some kind of circus performance, whilst the stretcher and child was slowly lowered from the ship's deck down to the waiting smaller boat that was waiting below. Once reaching land, an ambulance was on standby waiting to rush him up the hill to the hospital at Steamer Point as the emergency crew worked through the required procedures to establish how severe the injury was. Perhaps this was to be the end of the journey for the family, who knows. Their luggage was packed ready, just in case they needed to make some alternative arrangement for continuing the journey later after the ship had moved on with the remaining passengers.

As the x ray results came through there was a huge sigh of relief that was breathed by everyone, especially the family. There was no fracture discovered; however, the x ray clearly indicated that he had received a dent to his head in the process. The family was advised to be careful with him, but as the same child grew into adulthood, he was passed medically fit to take up a full career in the Royal Army, serving with the first battalion of the Royal Anglian regiment. However, during his military career, he was so pleased to be armed with this documentary evidence that would give some validity to his claim that he was not fit to obey the orders to join the boxing team, a sport that he was far from enamoured with.

Within the domain of domestic issues would come the far less dramatic occasions of caring for the children who took ill like any other child might and still requiring the very basics of a mothers tender loving care. Approaching the Suez Canal, the family prepared to go up on deck to see what sights were visible. All, that is, except for Violet and one of her young children. Even at sea, mothers have the task of nursing the sick children, and one of them had fallen ill with a chest infection and was confined to his bed in the cabin. He felt completely miserable; he would rather have been with the rest of the children. Violet had a very good interest in poetry, and made good use of her own personal expertise to write poetry. She wrote a poem especially for the invalid, and in between the entertaining of her young son she read to him the words she had written.

In the meanwhile, whilst the youngster had the attention of his own personal mummy, the rest had gathered on the deck looking for the Egyptian sights, perhaps even a pyramid or two, they had hoped. There was a measure of excitement that there may be a possibility of seeing these unique Egyptian historical sites. However, the traditional stone tombs for the Pharaohs were predominately built near the river Nile, for ease of transportation for the slaves of old who used the water to their advantage. As such, if this was all they looked for they would be destined to be hugely disappointed, there was not one mummy buried in sight of the Suez Canal. Not one pyramid could be seen within the horizon from any direction.

As the ship was navigated through the canal, there was a whole host of small boats that were seen to come out to meet them. The boats were full of merchants, each of them hoping to sell their tourist souvenirs to any who were wishing to purchase them. At that time it was a very lucrative place for the tradesmen vending their possessions from below the mighty ships of the sea. There were so many ships passing through the canal on route between the Far East and the United Kingdom, and many passengers appreciated the opportunity of making a purchase on the way, perhaps just one more souvenier before their sea journey was complete. It was quite an art to make the exchange of goods. A rope would be thrown from one vessel to the other, as money was conveyed down in one direction and the goods went up in the other direction. As the family returned to the cabin, they came armed with so many different souvenirs to boast of, including a stool that was designed to look like an ornamental camel. This was one souvenier that the family would keep as a treasured memory aid for many decades ahead.

Sometimes the voyages would have passed through the centre of international tensions. On another trip through the Suez Canal, there was not such a healthy welcome waiting for the ships that were travelling through, including theirs. The Gulf of Aden was shaped like a funnel with the Red Sea as its angled spout. As the day progressed ships going their way converged on the spout as their courses started lining up. With traffic coming out of the Red Sea as well, they were treated to more frequent and closer passings. The sea began changing colour too as it became more shallow, dropping to less than sixty metres. The water at that point was taking on just a hint of green in place of the opaque oceanic blue that they had become used to.

As they approached the Suez Canal they looked out at the Red Sea coast which was renowned for its incredible turquoise waters and splendid coral reefs. Everything seemed to be idyllic, until they reached the canal. President Nazzer, who was the political leader of Egypt at the time, was not feeling so very happy with the western countries whose ships were frequently travelling through. This time, there were no boats to be seen coming to meet them selling their wares. There were no longer any smiling cheerful faces to be appreciated, shouting the greetings and offering goods for sale.

They were replaced by something that was far more sinister and disturbing, experiences that were threatening, menacing and soon to spoil the hopes of a peaceful voyage, "Migs", or

"MiG-15's" to be more precise. These were the main stay of the Egyptian Air Force at the time, which were provided for them by the Soviet Union, the first assignment arriving in Egypt in nineteen fifty five. As the ship made its way along, the crew needed to possess nerves of Steel, as the Migs would carry out dive bombing exercises repeatedly without pulling the trigger or releasing its load. As the Migs dived down as close to the decks as was possible, the ship's captain gave the order for all passengers to go below decks immediately. Clearly, there was no intention for the pilots to cause any physical harm, but merely to scare them and cause the maximum amount of nuisance to the crew and passengers. However, despite all of the attempts that were made to cause disruption, the ship was still able to arrive at its final destination safe and sound.

On another occasion they were to be involved in a different form of intrigue. This time the ship was scheduled to call into Gibraltar, at the western entrance to the Mediterranean Sea. The family was looking forward to this, as it was one place they had not yet visited, but it was not going to be. Orders had come through for them to call by the island of Cyprus in the eastern end of the Mediterranean. It was night time as they arrived, and they anchored out at sea, nearby to the island. It was intended to be a secret rescheduling of the itinery, but it was certainly a last minute change. They waited as the signals went back and forth across the water. The passengers may not have been privy to all the details of what was happening, but they could see the signals being given and received as coded lights were exchanged between ship and shore.

It was during the times, prior to Cyprus independence, when the Eoka Greek Cypriot organisation was using all the means at their disposal to gain Independence. As the Morse code of flashing lights came to a close, the first of a batch of soldiers appeared having climbed on board from the small boat that had just approached the ship. One by one, they each took their place, lugging their kit bags along with them. Whatever the reason for this mini exodus, these soldiers had been detailed to become part of the body of Passengers that were travelling from Cyprus through to Southampton.

However, the long awaited visit into Gibraltar was never going to be. Cyprus was to be the one and only stopping place in the Mediterranean, with no opportunity for sightseeing or shopping for souveniers, merely the mystery of the boarding party of soldiers, and the secret scheming and plotting to ensure the soldiers were safely on board for the remainder of the journey. "The Mediterranean" only has one real meaning, but it has a lot of connotations. Hearing the word Mediterranean, a botanist will automatically think of the Mediterranean climate, found in other parts of the world like California. A historian will think of ancient cultures like the Phoenician, Egyptian, and Greek, as well as the Carthaginian or Roman civilizations. An architect, however, will imagine the Spanish tiled roofs or villas with arches, or perhaps he will envisage the Italian fishing villages scattered along the shore line. And so on. But for our travellers, there would now be other thoughts that would always permeate their memory.

It was in the month of October, in nineteen fifty eight, that the family would have boarded the Troop Ship Empire Fowey, and there is no doubt that as they did so they would have been wondering which of these kinds of adventures that they would be destined to be tasting the experience of as they began this voyage to the far side of the world. Travelling the world was certainly a means of seeing a variety of life's experiences, with awareness that each new day would inevitably bring new and interesting insights, that would realize a new knowledge to equip them in all that lay before them, and as such there could never be an excuse for complaining of boredom.

They had scrambled along the gang plank, and deposited the luggage in its appropriate place in the cabin. Then, before the ship set off, they would all have gathered together on deck, as did most of the other passengers that were sharing that journey, to bid farewell to Singapore. There were indeed many valuable memories of the island that would go with them. There were some extremely treasured times that had been shared together with some precious people. Some of the passengers would have friends below in the harbour that had come to bid farewell. They all waved towards each other, some would possibly have shed a tear or two as they reflected on the memories they were leaving behind, maybe even wishing that it might be possible to return, yet realising that the gangplank they had used to board the ship was very much a movable structure and the opportunity to change their minds concerning the voyage was no longer a viable option.

As they began the voyage leaving Singapore there would still be some wondrous sights for them to behold. They would look out and see the junks that were sailing beside them, still a common sight in the eastern waters well into the twentieth century, both in the deep oceans and rough seas as well as the more sheltered narrow inlets and rivers. These wooden Chinese sailing boats, with their high poop decks, were extremely beautiful to look at; often they were gaily painted, with their sails spread out with long flexible bamboo sticks. They were certainly not called junks because they were lousy, far from it. The word came not from China, but from a Malay word "jung" meaning "floating house".

To the one side would be the last sights of Singapore itself, bustling with the natural life growing from the fertile ground, with the vegetation and the foliage from the extensive range of flora that was growing right down to the water edge. The few native houses that would be scattered along the coastline added to the exquisite scenery that surrounded them. The beauty of these sights was what caught the eye of many as they arrived in Singapore, and now it was the last sights for them to remember

31

on their departure. The passengers would have been reflecting on all of these last thoughts and noting the nostalgic significance of it all for them realizing that this may well be the last sights of the island they had come to know as home.

Yet others would speak of something else that had caught the eye, not just the friends they knew who had come to wave good bye and shed a tear or two, or memories of the special times that they had shared, or even that special unique beauty of the island they were leaving behind. There was something more than that which had impressed them as they began the voyage, it was the sight and the sound of a huge choir of local Chinese people that had gathered together singing in English. They had gathered long before the gang plank was raised, and continued to be there as the ship moved out toward the horizon. Few could fail to be emotionally touched as they heard the voices harmoniously and clearly sing out the words, "God be with you till we meet again".

Some would enquire of each other as to who the choir could be, and who could the VIP be that's on board that would have been the reason for this grand choir to have gathered on the pier to sing as the Ship prepared to set sail. Violet smiled to herself, for she knew who the choir was, and who was on board that gave the reason for the choir to be there. The answers that Violet had would be the answers that would be the culmination of the story that lies in the coming pages. In the meanwhile, the words being heard were being sung so eloquently of the need of protection upon life's journey, something that one is only aware of fully when armed with hind sight.

God be with you till we meet again;
By His counsels guide, uphold you,
With His sheep securely fold you;
God be with you till we meet again.

Till we meet, till we meet,
Till we meet at Jesus' feet;
Till we meet, till we meet,
God be with you till we meet again.

God be with you till we meet again;
Neath His wings protecting hides you;
Daily manna still provides you;
God be with you till we meet again.

As she had listened to the singing, and as she heard the comments of her fellow passengers, Violet allowed her own thoughts to begin to drift back, reflecting upon the events that lay within this tour that had just been completed within Singapore. At this point in history, many of the local people in Singapore would have been looking forward with anticipation to the prospect of gaining self government in the coming year, this was to be their national "coming of age". But for Violet this was a time to look back with appreciation for the benefits of the past three years, and to use that time as a spring board for the future.

There was so much that had happened during this time, so much which had helped to enable her to understand more completely, in a deep and personal way just how much truth there was that lay within the words that were being sung in tuneful melodious voices by those who were congregated below, as well as being able to understand the reason for this grand choir being present on the quay side to bid farewell to those travelling on the Troop ship, Empire Fowey. Much had transpired during these past two and a half eventful years that had brought her to the realisation that she would never have reached this part of her journey of life if it were not for this same God that the choir was singing of, the one who had been with her every step along the way.

The poem written with a mother's love in the Suez - 2nd November 1958

A little child was ill one day,
He could not run & shout and play,
He had to stop upon his bed,
Because of a pain in his head.

He had a cough, it was so bad,
And he felt so ill & so sad:
He heard the wind so gay and free,
And said: "O wind, come talk to me."

The wind said "Little boy, I see
The waves playing so gay and free,
I hear the sound of music sweet,
The flowers dancing at my feet.

On the other side of the hill,
I turn the sail of the water mill,
And I shake the leaves in the tree:
And they come tumbling down to me.

Tomorrow I will blow and blow,
And all the hats, up, up, will go.
Then all the people leap and shout:
When I blow them all round about.

O little boy, now come with me,
And join the winds so gay and free.
And I will blow your pains away,
Then you will sing and shout all day."

V. A. Magee (1916 - 2009)

(Map showing Singapore)

CHAPTER 2

Memories are made of this?

As the year ninety fifty six appeared on the scene, the song "Memories are made of this" was climbing the record charts with the singer Dean Martin. In the same year as the recording, it was the memories that Singapore gave to the family that were to be most important to them. The singer may have spoken of his magic moments, but for the family the times on this island were the real special years of life, even if they were not inclined to phrase the word magic.

It was in nineteen fifty six, towards the beginning of the year, that the family had arrived on the island of Singapore following a long sea voyage. It was in nineteen fifty six that Britain abolished the death penalty, and it was the same year that the family anticipated the experience of abundance of tropical life. The island had already become a very familiar and enjoyable place to the family, having lived here previously and come to appreciate it as their own wonderfully unique "Paradise Island" which they had taken completely into the depth of their hearts.

Yes, it was a place where they could find such exotic wild life, but it was also seen as a personal "Garden of Eden" for them that encompassed the very essence of life itself, not so much a walled garden but nevertheless it was a Garden of Eden that was completely surrounded by the warm clear blue and green water in the tropical eastern world. Singapore was situated almost on the Equator, which meant it was a hot and humid climate all year round. There was more rain fall from the month of November till January, with July being the driest month.

It was Mark Twain that had once wisely said "twenty years from now you will be more disappointed by the things you did not do than by the things you did do .... Explore, dream". Likewise, it was Eleanor Roosevelt who said "The future belongs to those who believe in the beauty of their dreams".

With such a philosophy to life there must be so much for them to dream of as they explored the possibilities, seeking out every aspect that would enhance their lives. Singapore was in many ways an interesting place to be, not in the least due to its multi-cultural and multi-ethnic population and was an excellent destination for those people who were wishing to have a taste of south East Asia. The Singaporeans were a mix of mainly Chinese, Malay, Indian and Eurasian people. Singapore's history was indeed a rich tapestry, weaving the cultural influences that came from the Malay Archipelago, China and India. In everything from architecture to food, holidays to languages, Singapore was a small island that celebrated the ways in which diversity had enriched its heritage and continued to play a leading role in its development.

Some of these various racial groups had been living in Singapore for many generations. All in all this made Singapore a very interesting place! If there could be one word that would best capture the spirit of Singapore it would have to be the word unique. A dynamic place that was rich both in colour and contrast, it had a harmonious blend of culture, cuisine and arts, and was brimming with such unbridled energy.

Like an emergent butterfly, the delicate beauty of the Insect Kingdom of the island also promised to be breath taking! Reflecting back they all knew how much they had already been dazzled by the riot of colours and thousands of tiny wings that would be fluttering freely past them as they strolled through some of the natural environments of these fragile specimens of natural life. Singapore had a number of specific attractions that would keep even the most restless person entertained for days. Singapore could keep the family perpetually entertained with its unique beauty and unbridled energy.

This was to be the third occasion that the family had lived on the island of Singapore, and was also memorable as the birth place for one of the six children of the family, Geraldine, who was born at the Royal Air Force hospital in the east of the island at Changi in March nineteen fifty, and as such the family had been given the opportunity to become well acquainted with all of the delights and wonders that were an integral part of the island life they would be experiencing. They could even look back on the excursion they had taken as a family across the causeway into Malaya, and the delightful visit they experienced going to the Sultan of Jahores private zoo. They could also see the Singapore railway station, with its rotund clock hanging outside. This was the place where many would have nervously boarded the train for an often perilous journey up through Malaya.

Then there were also the visits to Haw Par Villa, or "Tiger Balm Gardens" as it was also known as. The gardens were full of tableaux of garishly coloured cement animals and figures, revealing various Chinese myths and recreations of folklore and moral tales. Haw Par Villa was the quintessential house of the Chinese folklore. Described by various visitors as being "fascinating, delightful, bizarre and entertaining", Haw Par Villa was considered by many to be like no other place seen in the world. Some would also always remember the gruesome models of people depicting the punishments they went through following their death and transition through Hades, the kind of images that would be inclined to create such horrendous nightmares for many a child after visiting the garden.

The gardens were created in nineteen thirty seven by the entrepreneurial and charismatic Aw Boon Haw as a gift for his brother Aw Boon Par, and they both hoped that it would be used as a venue for teaching traditional Chinese values. It was certainly unique in its character and rich in heritage and educational values. They had worked on the philosophy "that which is derived from society should be returned to society", their motto for life. Aw Boon Haw was the millionaire owner of the Tiger Balm medical ointment which was used for aches, pains and, most important in the tropics, mosquito bites.

However, there were still such tremendous possibilities that lay before them as they arrived at this tropical island in the sun and they were prepared to make the most of every opportunity that was given to them. Previously the family had resided in other districts of the island, at Tengah and Seletah, but this time Paddy had been given a posting to a different part of the island, as he took up the position he was appointed to at the Royal Air Force hospital at Changi, the same establishment where his own daughter had been born in some years previously.

Changi itself was a very idyllic area where there were very few buildings and those that were there were mostly quaint, old and low rise buildings. The Changi roads were much narrower than most and were lined with palm trees. In the sixteen hundred's, Changi was called Tanjung Rusa. Tanjung Rusa was then later renamed Tanjung Changi at some point in the eighteen hundred's. The name 'changi', like many other of the district names in Singapore, was derived from the name of a plant that was abundant in the area. However, nobody was sure exactly which plant 'changi' referred to, or even how the district came to be named as such. What people did discover, however, was that Changi had become an ideal venue for picnics as they enjoyed the natural environment and the warm weather.

It would soon become evident to the family, however, that this particular visit to Singapore was destined to become one that certainly would begin with a lot of stress and strain for everyone, despite all the pleasures of this island paradise they had come to know which filled them with such excitement and elation. However, what would be the conclusion of the visit? What was the secret of life that would manage to lift them up and support them through all of the difficult and extreme experiences that they would discover around them? Where would they find the support that they could feel would carry them onto the next stage of the journey of life? Succeeding in the marathon that is known as the journey of life is always dependent on these kinds of vital questions being adequately answered.

As a family they had to face issues they may have hoped to have left behind them during the war. There would be the time when the news came through that a family friend who was a pilot had crashed in the jungle. As time went by, and no sighting of him was found his family were told he was reported as being "missing, presumed dead". As a family friend they had shared so much together, and felt the pain of it all as if he was family. Fortunately he was eventually found by some friendly natives, who cared for him and ensured he was brought safely back to civilization alive and well. Paddy was also able to reflect on the time he rushed out to the airfield as he saw an aircraft crashing on a separate occasion. He was the first one there, but there was little he could do, the pilot was already dead on the site. However, there was to be more than these incidents during this tour to bring the added stress to life.

They were arriving on the island on this occasion during a period of extreme political uncertainty that was following close after a war in which another eastern country in Asia, namely Japan, had revealed that the "mighty" western powers can be just as vulnerable as any other nation or race of the world, and therefore could be challenged to seek out the vulnerability of this colonial power. Although the British had been welcomed back into the community of Singapore after the war, the fact remained in the eyes of some that the British had failed to defend them adequately in their time of need. It was the view of many of the Singaporeans that this had cost them their credibility as being infallible rulers. The decades after the war saw a political awakening amongst the local populace and the rise of nationalistic and anti-colonial sentiments. Hence, the Japanese Occupation was to be the cause of the path to eventual independence to be greatly accelerated, as the local public confidence in the ability of their British leaders in protecting them crumbled.

The Chinese riots became a significant and disruptive feature of the decade of the nineteen fifties. These would have initially started with what was to become known as the Hock Lee bus riots, which occurred on the twelfth of May in nineteen fifty five. Four people were killed and thirty one others were injured in the violence that ensued. Earlier, on the twenty third of April, nineteen fifty five, workers from the Hock Lee Amalgamated Bus Company and some Chinese students began to go on strike. They believed that they had a genuine grievance, and therefore expected the authorities to greatly respect their concerns. They were members of the Singapore Bus Workers' Union, or the SBWU as they were known to some through the initials of the union, and were protesting against the poor working conditions they had been experiencing, along with long working hours and low pay.

The situation was also further aggravated by the fact that they also felt threatened by a rival union which was supported by the bus company to counter any labour action by the SBWU. The strike was rumoured to have been instigated by pro-communist agitators. However, despite all of the idle speculation that was

41

circulating in the locality, it was more likely to have been fanned by the anti-colonial sentiments, as emotions became more intense and volatile through a period of time.

In nineteen fifty six, there began what was to become known as the Chinese middle school riots. The Chinese middle schools riots were a series of riots that broke out in the Singapore community, resulting in thirteen people being killed and more than one hundred people being injured. It was in nineteen fifty six, after Lim Yew Hock replaced David Marshall as the Chief Minister of Singapore, that he began to take tough and challenging measures that were envisaged to be the means of suppressing any communist activities that might have taken place. He took such action with the full support and cooperation of the British Governor and the Commissioner of Police.

Though Singapore was a British colony there was still a system of organisation that was accountable within its own locality. The origins of the public bureaucracy in Singapore could actually be traced back to its founder, Stamford Raffles, who had initiated the tradition of a completely separate civil service by establishing the nucleus of the civil service through the appointment of his deputy, Major Farquhar, as the Resident, his brother-in-law as the Master Attendant, and four other officials in eighteen nineteen.

In September, Lim Yew Hock then deregistered and banned two pro-communist organizations: the Singapore Women's Association, which was otherwise known as the S.W.A., and also the Chinese Musical Gong Society. The Chinese Middle School Students Union, or the S.C.M.S.S.U., was also dissolved by the Chief Minister and he banished two Chung Cheng High School teachers. Under his direction, the Special Branch also detained Chia Ek Tian, a leading trade unionist who was considered to be responsible for the plans for an uprising against the British, though ironically Lim Yew Hock was himself a trade unionist prior to entering politics.

In protest, the students had gathered and camped at the Chung Cheng High School and also at the Chinese High School. They staged a "sit in" over the next two weeks, organising meetings and holding a number of public demonstrations. On the twenty fourth of October, sensing that urgent action was required to be taken, the government issued an ultimatum that the schools were to be vacated. As the deadline for the ultimatum approached, riots started initially at the Chinese High school and then spread to other parts of the island. Conflict now appeared to have become a matter that was inevitable as each sought to challenge each other.

In a show of support and encouragement, students had arrived in bus loads to join those who had been striking and protesting. They organised donation drives, brought food and money, and even entertained the workers with songs and dances and cabaret acts. As they would pass any Europeans that may have been taking the same route along the way the family recalled how the demonstrators had made the show of holding their noses with one hand, whilst using the other hand to make a movement up and down as if pulling a chain that would be the usual function of that time to flush the toilets. This juvenile "game of charades" was intended to be considered an insult that would perhaps goad the Europeans into an angry response to these attempts to humiliate them, but in reality most people treated the demonstration as merely a childish joke that was not worthy of any retaliation from them in any way. Maybe it was equally a cause of considerable annoyance to the demonstrators that the Europeans would laugh back at them loudly, rather than expressing any offence at the action.

Initially, the family were resident in a place that was known as Katong, a residential district that lay in the east end of the island, which was out with of the military base and therefore providing a far less secure living accommodation during the times of unrest such as this. Some of the students and other rioters were known to gather as a crowd nearby, shouting out various words of insult to any of the British population who were anywhere within earshot. They were taunting them, goading them, seeking any kind of reaction, whilst they armed themselves with metal dust bin lids, which they would bang together as loudly as possible.

The intention was to try and instil a sense of fear, alarm and despondency amongst the young families of the servicemen that lived in the locality, and in the process undermine the morale of the whole of the British community. It was a tremendous racket, as the noise seemed to get increasingly louder and louder, reverberating as it impacted and pounded into the depths of their minds. There seemed as if there was no sanctuary available, no peace and shelter from the mounting tension that surrounded them as the noise echoed from house to house and back again. There was no part of their housing that would be discovered to give a haven against the invasion of the noise.

It was at that time that two soldiers gave a loud knock at the door of the family home; amazingly it was a knock that was even louder than the noise outside. Many of the husbands were stuck on the base, unable to get home due to the severity of the troubles that had flared up throughout the length of the island, or else they were required to carry out essential duties. The soldiers sought to console the wives and children, assuring them that they had no need to worry, as they would be in safe hands because they were patrolling the houses throughout the night, as their duty required.

If they heard anyone or noticed anything that was remotely suspicious, they said, do not open the door to check what it might be, whatever the circumstances may be. They also advised that there may be attempts to trick people into opening the door, perhaps by using some clever pretext. No matter how genuine a caller may appear to be, they said; the door must never be opened through the night under any circumstances. Instead they were advised to just keep flashing the house lights on and off and they would come round to assist them as soon as possible. This, they said, was a solemn promise they could depend upon. It would appear to be a simple yet effective improvised alarm system accessible to every resident in the housing scheme. However, there was little comfort left with the family as the men left and moved on to the next house to repeat exactly the same words of assurance.

Violet had listened to them, but said nothing, keeping her own counsel on the matter. Just one look at these men and she was quickly aware that their offer of help would be extremely limited, no matter how hard they would try and how genuine were their intentions. As they had gone from house to house, they had been offered expressions of gratitude for the offer of assistance and support, along with another welcome gift of a glass of beer, or perhaps some other alcoholic refreshment. By this time, Violet thought, they do not look capable of supporting each other, let alone anyone else who might face a time of crisis through the long dark night that lay before them. Hope did not seem to emerge easily from what the men had said because their appearance did not match up with their words.

Here was the essence of the difference that lay between being hopeful and feeling hopeless, a difference that depended upon the amount of confidence one can have within a promise. A promise means very little if there are no indications that confidence can be matched with the words that are given. How much worse could things become by the time the night is completed? They were left with the feeling that they were going to be left completely on their own, isolated, whatever transpired through the night. There was no encouragement left for any of them and it seemed like their whole world had collapsed. It was Oscar Wilde that once said "The world is a stage, but the play is badly cast." However, people forget to their peril that they are the cast that needs to get the lines and the action right. This was one of those moments that everyone in the cast needed to be depended upon.

As the family prepared to go to their beds, they each decided to choose something that they could put under their pillow, something that could be used as a means of defence, just in case it was required to give them some protection against any unwelcome intruder that might appear during the middle of the night. The concept of children taking a "comforter" to bed with them at night seemed to be gaining a completely different concept as the family made their own plans for protection and reassurance of personal security. Desperate times require desperate measures if they were all to be kept safe, they reasoned, as they chose the items that they felt could instil the vital confidence that had been failing in the promises they had received earlier in the day from those representing the security forces. One of them would have had a toy gun; another would have a rolling pin, whilst one even had a large carving knife to put under the pillow.

How they had expected to use them was a mystery even to them, and yet in some uncanny way, knowing that the weapons were present and available close by seemed to be sufficient to instil within them the reassurance that did not seem to materialise with the soldiers that had called by earlier. If they needed any help, they were sure that they would be best protected if they were self supporting, there was nothing else left, it seemed, for them to place their confidence in. Despite all the preparations they had made for their security, sleep did not come easy to them that night as they saw the minute hand on the clock tick through every moment that passed. Each of them would be imagining the possibilities of how things could turn out should they need to protect themselves against such an unwelcome visitor. With some of the weapons they had chosen, it could turn out to be quite a blood thirsty night if any intruder dared to face up to this homemade arsenal, with many tears likely to be shed by the end of the conflict. Such details were not going to be the making for "sweet dreams", more likely they would be disturbing nightmares being experienced as they would toss and turn from one direction to another. Peaceful slumbers were not going to come easy for any of them as they watched the hands of the clock move from one minute to another, one hour to another.

It was the middle of the night when all of their worst fears appeared to be realised. They all heard the noises at the same moment, as they moved slowly and quietly out of their rooms with their chosen weapons in their hands, ready for action. They looked at each other in the eyes, and in some distinct way seemed to recognise the concerned thoughts of the other, as they discerned the presence out with of someone they had not invited to be with them. In silence, not a word being spoken, they were aware of the feelings of fear being expressed by each of them in the body language they revealed. In the stillness of the dark night, the noises always seem to travel further, and in the darkness, fears always seem greatest.

They began whispering to each other, realising that someone was outside of their own front door. Who could it be? What were his intentions? What were they to do in response? What could they do? Could there be something they might be able to consider doing to pre-empt the intentions of the intruder lurking around outside? There were so many questions that were coming to mind, but where were the answers to be found? One of them called across to their mother, Violet, to say she had her sharp carving knife at hand, should she open the door to see who was there. "No", said Violet, "you heard the instructions that the two soldiers gave to us earlier today, just keep to the directions that were given for now. Just remain quiet, stay calm, and keep the door locked whilst we summon help by flashing the lights on and off." That would, at the least, be an action that would keep the children occupied whilst Violet thought about what they might be able to do next. It seemed like an age had passed as the lights were flashed, but no help emerged, not one genuine offer of assistance arrived. As Violet had feared, the protectors must have had one glass too many and were possibly collapsed in some remote corner until the effects of the alcohol they had consumed had worn off. They were now completely on their own; there was no one available to back them up, no protection to assist them in their moment of vulnerability.

Together they would need to discover what would be the best way to support and protect each other. It was looking like a very steep learning curve that they would all need to go through before day light should arrive, but there was little choice available for them in the matter. The safe keeping of them all has to depend upon such solidarity because no one else was available for them. No one dared to imagine what the consequences could be by the time morning emerged if they did not make the correct decisions concerning their response to the danger that lay around them. The grasping of valuable wisdom was paramount to the aspirations of the keeping of their lives in safety.

They could still hear the noises that were coming from outside the house, whoever was there had not moved on yet and did not appear to have any intentions of doing so, and as such the intruders remained as a potential and dangerous threat to their security. The whole episode was becoming increasingly alarming as the time passed by. Someone was actually trying the front door handle, even if they were unsuccessful in opening the door. Fear was now gripping each of the children as they contemplated all of the prospects that could materialize. Violet decided the best way forward now was to attempt to bluff the way out of the situation as she considered the well being of each of her young family. She called through the front door, "Go away, we are well armed in here, and we have others coming to help any moment now." Surely, she thought that should scare them off, whoever they might be.

However, to her surprise and personal disturbance it had not scared them in the least. Violet was shocked as she heard the voice of the man on the outside; he was still there and persistently continuing to have just one thing in mind. "Let me in," the voice on the outside called, "I need to get in, unlock and open up the door quickly." It was not a very loud voice, but it was definitely the voice of a man, and one who had clearly got some boldness to assume he could demand his way into her house and expect her to agree without any resistance. Violet knew that she needed to match that boldness with as much inner courage as she could manage to muster, no matter how difficult that may be, if she was to manage to do her best for the children. If only Paddy was here to support them, she thought to herself, but that was not to be. He had his work to do, and she had to be the one who was there to keep the family safe

In the meanwhile, Paddy had been working hard at his place of work, the hospital. In nineteen twenty six, the plantations and coastal cliffs off Changi had been cleared to make way for an air base and the six story buildings that were eventually to become a hospital. The area was mainly to be used for military barracks and administrative quarters by the British, who built an airbase, a prison and eventually a hospital for military personnel. These places were still standing, and were likely to be long after the British would leave the island. Changi Hospital itself, where Paddy was working, functioned as the primary British military hospital providing medical care for all British servicemen stationed in the Eastern part of Singapore, and as such it had a crucial role to play should there be any casualties arising out of the riots that took place, or any other incidents that may have materialized.

Following the clearance of the land, the hospital itself was built in the nineteen thirties, and had quite an interesting and rich history that had spanned throughout the war and the Japanese occupation. In the initial plans it was not meant to be a hospital when it was first built, that was to be developed later. The British were planning to have a heavily guarded military location in the east of Singapore. The site was strategically selected as it was high on top of a hill overlooking the sea surrounding most of the east side and the south side of the island. Therefore, it was even at this point in its history crucially based for security purposes.

His duties and responsibilities for the day had now been finally completed to his satisfaction, and so Paddy had absolutely nothing to do now except find a comfortable bed to sleep in for the night. He was exhausted, and therefore this final task of the day was essential if he was ever likely to be able to give his best to his work and assignments for the next day. There was no exaggeration to say that one of the most beautiful scenes in Singapore could be seen from the hospital. Facing east, it was possible to grasp the first beam of morning sun ray high on the roof top. Magnificent views of such places as Jahore that was situated on the southern tip of the Malayan peninsular and Puala Ubin could also be seen from there in a way that could never be seen elsewhere on the island. The sights were amazing. Tremendous as the views may have been, however, that is possibly the last thing one thinks of when completing a long and tiring shift knowing that there was no possibility for him of heading back to relax in the family home. He had no idea when normal family life could be realistically envisaged for him though he still hoped that it would be a dream that would soon be realized.

Realising that there did not appear to be going to be any chance of him getting home that night, however, he prepared to walk across to the sergeant's mess and make a reservation for his accommodation. Yet as if in contrast his thoughts would keep drifting to his hopes of getting home. At times he could sense a gentle breeze wafting along the corridor, which was quite refreshing after a long hot day. It was at that moment that he met up with his friend, who was clearly geared up for a trip somewhere. A special operations convoy was being arranged to Katong. This seemed like an opportunity that was far too good for him to lose out on. There were no passengers that would be allowed to go with them, but Paddy soon picked up on the fact that they were one man short for the convoy. This had to be more than a coincidence. Could this be his chance to get home for the night after all? He desperately hoped that it was a possibility, though realising that it would be a highly unlikely option for him. However, he sensed it was important to keep a positive outlook on the whole matter. Hope would always burn on the fuel of a positive mentality, but never on a negative outlook.

He knew he was not qualified for this particular assignment that was being discussed, the most specific reason being that he was meant to be a non combatant due to him serving as a part of the medical team at the hospital. However, it was to his advantage that he possessed a natural Irish ability to talk himself into or out of any given situation when he wished to do so, often claiming to have kissed the proverbial Irish Blarney stone. To kiss the Blarney Stone was said to bring about a charm on the kisser, to bestow upon them a silver tongue with which to spin tales and songs to mesmerize others. In addition to that, it was his friend who was organising the details of the expedition, and what were friends for if it were not to help each other out when they were in times of desperate need. Such a time as this was surely a moment of desperate need.

It was to be an armed convoy as there were expected to be so many risks to contend with along the way as they travelled through the night. Paddy, having received the appropriate letters of authority, began to draw out his rifle and ammunition from the armoury, and made his way to the assembly point. From there, they would begin the long drive down the hill, and on into the night. As he took up his position he was aware that though he had been issued with this weapon, he did not have a clue what to do with it if the situation required it. He was, as such, a liability to the team should there be any emergency to deal with. Talking is sometimes so much easier than doing. As a non combatant he was possibly breaking every rule that was known to be in the book, every possible regulation that covered the situation, but at this moment in time he was far from caring whether he was breaking any rules or regulations or not as they advanced closer by the mile to the place that he had come to know as his home.

It was pitch dark outside as they travelled along the route, and it was virtually impossible for any of them to see adequately as they endeavoured to keep looking out for any possible concerns that may have surrounded them. During the day light, this road would have revealed how much of a transformation had taken place on the island since the time when Sir Thomas Stamford Bingley Raffles realised the full potential that the island had for the British influence in the region. Sir Thomas Raffles had bought the island on behalf of Queen Victoria for a mere one hundred pounds, sterling, at the beginning of the nineteenth century as part of a strategy to contend with the Dutch presence in the nearby Dutch East Indies, or Indonesia as it would be referred to at a later date.

The price that he paid was an unbelievable bargain, it was ridiculously low, but at that time no one wanted the island, not having the essential visionary fore sight they could not appreciate its full worth. They never understood the depth of its capacity for development as it was not much more than a huge swamp land plagued with malaria carrying mosquitoes, and what can one do with a swamp. They envisaged nothing of the capabilities that would come to the naturalists mind. Sir Thomas Raffles, however, who was a naturalist, was able to visualise how much could grow out of an island that appeared to be of no use to anyone else. In eighteen twenty he was to declare *"My Settlement of Singapore continues to thrive most wonderfully - it is all and everything I could wish and, if no untimely fate awaits it, promises to become the Emporium and the pride of the East"* . Raffles had very clear ideas about the kind of town he wanted to establish: shipping on the river, Chinatown on the right bank (he called it the "Chinese cam pong," using the Malay word for village), a government area on the left bank--and, beyond it, what he called the "European town." Still farther out, there would be an "Arab cam pong." All were to lie on neatly gridded streets.

This was to be the beginnings of the formal presence on the island being formed by the British colonialists, and the establishment of the City of Singapore. Things within the region were to advance considerably in the times that lay ahead, because Raffles established his trading centre on an island that was covered with tropical forests and ringed with mangrove swamps. As someone once said, "........ Without vision the people perish", with vision the horizons will expand considerably.

((Statue of Sir Thomas Raffles)

Since then the entire island had been completely transformed, having been drained and irrigated and made economically viable. Plant life was established, much of it tropical, and as one looked around it was possible to see banana trees, with their Broad, long, graceful leaves, or the Papaya, with its hollow green or deep purple trunk, or perhaps the coconut palm trees, and even rubber tree plantations. The rubber trees had originated in South America, where the British had acquired seeds which they germinated and then took to Ceylon for further development, and then in eighteen seventy seven began the plantations in Singapore. But none of the magnificent beauty of the scenery could be seen at this moment, indeed, to some degree the surrounding trees were themselves the means of creating an even greater darkness on the road as they clouded over what little light may have existed along the road. They were soon realising how dangerous the road was as they occasionally needed to quickly take evasive action with little warning on the road, but still they persevered with the mission they had in hand.

Occasionally the moon light would flicker through the foliage, giving them quick glimpses of what lay around them within the eerie silvery light, even if the light was shining unsteadily. It was in the midst of one of those quick glimpses that the driver was to inexplicably quickly slam on the brakes of his vehicle which was leading the military convoy as he attempted an emergency stop, resulting in the vehicle skidding and spinning dangerously out of control into the verge on the side of the road. Paddy lay briefly on his side in agony, the rifle having dug deep into his arm, causing an unbearable and unpleasant pain that was proving to be extremely difficult to tolerate.

However, whatever the pain may be, or how devastated each of the men may have been as a result of the incident, the primary task for them all was to inspect the reason for the driver putting on his brakes on this dark and dimly lit road. The occupants of the other vehicles quickly came forward to assist, whilst some of the party stood guard in case there should be any one around to cause further trouble. They had been very fortunate, it appeared. The quick thinking, and sharp reaction, of the driver had certainly saved them all from an even worse fate. In front of them lay a huge tree that covered the full width of the road.

On closer examination, it was clear that it could not have been possible for it to have fallen down on its own, but had been given some human assistance. There was no doubt that this had resulted from the endeavours of someone who had used some kind of saw to ensure that it fell down strategically across the road. The signs were all there, displayed in the markings on the trunk of the tree. They looked around by the side of the road, searching for any other booby traps or even some suspicious looking culprits that could have concealed themselves somewhere in the surrounding undergrowth, but whoever had been responsible for the incident had left the vicinity long ago. Once again, they had been very fortunate on this occasion, for things could have been far more severe if any of the demonstrators had remained nearby to continue and complete the plot they had planned together. The prospects within such a scenario would have been extremely unpleasant for the members of the convoy and the resulting consequences were too much for them to think about in the middle of the night.

During this time, it had become a common practice amongst those who wished to express their dissatisfaction with the British colonisation to cut the trees down in this fashion with two intentions in mind. First of all, it was hoped that the British vehicles would hit the fallen tree, which would result in the vehicle turning over on its side causing at least some injuries to the occupants. Secondly, whilst they were incapacitated in this manner the protestors who had been responsible for this felled tree would be waiting close by in hiding. Unseen to the victims, they were ready to bombard the occupants with stones, or anything else that they may be able to grab hold of and use as dangerous missiles to devastating effect, whilst the victims of the onslaught were unable to find shelter or protection from the onslaught that rained upon them. As such, it was a far more dangerous situation that had been planned for the party that night. However, on this occasion they had evidently decided it had become too late to wait any longer to see who they might find as the next victim. There was not one protester in sight they noted, as they breathed a huge sigh of relief that their fate was better than could have been.

The men gathered around in a group and grabbed every conceivable item that they could have envisaged as being usable as a tool to assist, and together, with such resourcefulness and initiative, they worked as a team, seeking to remove the obstacle that was hindering the movement of the convoy as quickly as they could manage. Some of the other vehicles would have been rigged up with a tow bar, which would have been ideal at this time to pull parts of the tree away as they used all of the resources available to clear the road that lay ahead of them.

Having removed the obstruction to the road, the next step was to ensure the vehicle that had skidded was sufficiently road worthy and put back onto the road for the remaining journey. Eventually, the task was completed, as they threw themselves down completely exhausted, back inside the vehicles that they had previously been driving. No matter how exhausted they may have been, however, the luxury of continuing to rest in the vehicles was not an option that was available to them this time. Now the road was clear they had to move on before any further dangers could arise. With considerable more care and attention and alertness, they continued further on the journey into Katong, their final destination, and their sights set firmly on home.

It was extremely late by the time that the convoy had arrived.

Paddy, with some measure of difficulty, slowly and carefully got out of the vehicle he had been travelling in, and made his way towards his home. Some degree of first aid had been hurriedly administered to his injured arm by his colleagues, but the pain was still there to be experienced, and the agony was showing little indication that it would ease away quickly. Every step resulted in further jarring of his injury; every motion was a movement further into his personal distress.

He cautiously made his way around the corner with some concerns as to how things have been for everyone in his absence, anxiously hoping that he had arrived home before any problems may have arisen and that he would find his family were truly safe and well. Stories had circulated of the intentions of the demonstrators toward the British families and his hopes were that such stories would not involve his own family, but he also knew that his concerns could have some genuine foundation. He knew there were risks for his family alone whilst he obeyed orders, but he was also hoping that the military had the fore sight to set up sufficient means to ensure support for all of the families, unaware of how disastrous such intentions had turned out to be amongst the drink fuelled soldiers. Of course, that was not the fault of the authorities themselves, but to those on the spot who were both the tempted and the tempters.

He was troubled within himself about having to leave them all alone and isolated whilst there was so much danger around, but it would also seem to him that he had been left with very little choice in the matter. The circumstances, along with the orders he was required to obey, dictated how things had to be whether he liked it or not. With the injuries he had sustained he was not too sure how much help he would be for them. Nevertheless, if there should be any intruders he felt equally confident that it would make a huge difference for the family to know that there was a man in the house now who could take a lead in ensuring the security of them all. Without his presence he was confident that no one would know what to do. The big question to answer was whether he had arrived in time for them all.

He hoped that he could make his way in without disturbing anyone, though he did not think through the possibility that his arrival unannounced into a darkened room may in itself have been a shock to his family, not realising who may be coming in. This was particularly the case in the early hours of the morning. However, in his weakened state there were occasions when he would inadvertently have knocked against various items that would have been laid in the way, and with the path being so dark it did not assist him too much in his endeavours to approach the house quietly. Sometimes he would have stumbled and fallen along the way, and then he would recover, and rise onto his feet again, one more time, staggering from one direction to another. Perseverance was essential if he would expect to have any realistic hope of reaching his goal for the night. Step by step, he aspired falteringly towards the front entrance.

Eventually he reached the front door and sought, unsuccessfully, to find his keys in his pocket, using the hand that was attached to his arm that was not injured, but the keys were not there. What was he to do? The keys he needed must be in the pocket on the other side, he thought to himself. How was he ever going to manage to reach the keys in the other pocket with an injured arm on that side? It was surely a terrible conundrum to overcome, he had discovered, and one to which he could envisage no possible solution. He struggled and wriggled in all kinds of directions, but no success emerged from his quest. The keys were unattainable. His frustration was building up within him, increasingly sensing his anger with his whole personal situation.

He sat down on the outside step as he sought to discover an appropriate answer to his situation, whilst at the same time he also gained a valuable opportunity to rest and recharge his weakened batteries. It had been a very long and eventful night, one he would not like to repeat in a hurry, but surely the end to it all must be nigh. He certainly hoped so. Through all that had happened that night he had been considerably weakened, but once he was back with the family he was confident that it would all have been worthwhile. He could visualise for a moment the comfort that lay before him, his tired feet elevated up as he recovered from his ordeal, puffing on the pipe and tobacco he loved to smoke.

It was at this moment that a most amazing thing happened that took him completely by surprise; the house lights began to flash on and off at a rapid speed. What could possibly be happening? If Paddy had been weak and confused before, then at this point he was considerably more confused, unable to think or reason clearly as to what he should be doing. The flashing lights were not helping him at all, in fact they were resulting in adding to his state of confusion, and they appeared to continue to flash for what seemed like an eternity. He desperately wished they would stop, but his wish was not being realised very quickly.

It was at that point that he heard Violets voice as she called out to him, "Go away, we are well armed in here, and we have others coming to help any moment now." Could that really be his Violet, who was saying those words to him? She was extremely small, petite, standing less than five feet tall, yet here she was sounding quite menacing as her voice boomed out loudly with her threats directed against him. Where did she manage to summon that loud voice from? He found it hard to believe that his own wife could be speaking like that to him. She was sounding so threatening to him.

That was some welcome after all he had experienced, he thought, not at all what he had been expecting as he set off on his incredible journey to support his family. He had thought that he would have been warmly welcomed with open and loving arms, but at least some one in the house is awake and perhaps they could open up the door for him, despite the apparent threats that were being issued. That would at least be one answer to the difficulties he was experiencing with finding the keys. He summoned up all the inner strength that he could manage to muster, and then with a weakened voice he called out, "Let me in, I need to get in, unlock and open up the door quickly." It was Paddy's voice that Violet had been hearing in the middle of the night, but in his weakened condition his voice was not recognisable to the family that were within the house.

"Why should I want to let you in?" asked Violet, "Who do you think you are?" It was very presumptuous of this mysterious person that was on the other side of the door to assume that he could just demand an entrance into her home, she thought to herself, in fact it was downright arrogant. If Violet had been shocked before, it did not compare with the shock of hearing the next words that came through the locked door, "Violet, it's me, Paddy, let me in quickly. I have been injured; I need to get in quickly. I am about to collapse if I stay out here much longer". She could not believe that it was her own husband she had been threatening. Still feeling a bit unsure and with a measure of caution, Violet opened the door slowly, and nervously, and saw for herself, it really was Paddy, and apparently there was no other danger that could be seen surrounding them. There was nothing to fear. As the door opened, so Paddy stumbled in through the entrance and collapsed in exhaustion once he was inside the house.

And where were those courageous soldiers, those men who had boldly declared their assurances that they would instantaneously be there as the fearless protectors whenever they got the signal given by the house lights being flashed on and off? Well, despite all of the fine categorical promises they were never to be seen again. There was no reliable defence for the family that night, not one person they were able to trust except for what they could provide for themselves. Presumably the "brave" men were still sleeping off the alcohol in some secluded and comfortable corner of the housing scheme and the courageous actions they spoke of remained captured in the bottom of the empty bottle, never to be retrieved again. The absolute and explicit words of assurance that had been given were, by themselves, not much help when it came to seeking to give some calming peace of mind concerning the security of these "helpless" families who were all alone and separated at the time from the "head of the family".

As they say, actions will always speak louder than words, but it seemed as if it was only words that were given to these vulnerable families that night, at least that was the perception of those who were anxiously waiting in vain for a response in the middle of the night, unsure of how the dangers of the night would develop. Uncertain as to whether they would ever see the welcome dawn of another day again, how many other families had hoped for the presence of the soldiers? However, as an old African proverb wisely declares, "no matter how long the night may be, there is always a dawn at the end". In other words, no matter how bad life may appear to be for any one of us, it is always important to keep open the belief that there is hope waiting to be realised for the future. Such a concept keeps everything in its proper perspective.

It was approximately at this period of time that the British servicemen on the island were informed that the school buses had ceased to be an appropriate regular means of transportation for their own children to use as they travel school. Concerns were expressed by the authorities concerning the safety of the British children in the midst of the riots that had become so prevalent at the time, and the buses were no longer seen as being a viable and secure means of transporting the youngsters to and from school.

As the children gathered in wait of the transport coming to take them to school, it was with considerable excitement as they found that they would need to clamber onto the back of an open top lorry, or as some would call them, the grey Gharry's. At the age they were, thoughts of the security reasons that lay behind the transportation decision would not be uppermost in the mind in any way. All that mattered was that going to school was now something they could look forward to with excitement, an unusual concept for most school children to comprehend, but they were living in unusual times. Sitting on the benches that were lined facing inward from the sides there were clear reminders here of the way the old parachute seats were positioned, as they imagined the parachuting experiences as being their own. It appeared to them to be a new adventure in life for them to experience, one that was to bring such a thrill, a sense of elation, as they now soared to new extreme levels of emotional expression.

For those who were so young that they were just starting primary school, it would have been a considerable height for them to climb up; perhaps feeling that it was much akin to mountaineering for those who were of small stature at this point in their lives, but without the need of carrying a map and compass. However, help was always available for them to ensure that nobody was feeling left out, as the younger children were lifted on board, or assisted in the climb up. Some would occasionally be offered the added treat of sitting in the cabin next to the driver. Jonathan had to wait for such exciting expeditions on the way to school, but his turn would come when he started school for the first time in the September, just prior to his fifth birthday in the December. By this time the family had moved to Haig road, which was closer to the school at Changi, but was still a distance that required transportation.

Covering the framework over the back of the lorry would be a system of netting that was designed to strongly resist any rocks, stones or any other dangerous items that may have been thrown like missiles aimed at the moving target, whilst still permitting the cooler breezes to blow through as the vehicle moved along and thereby ensure some valuable comfort for the children. This would not be as important early in the morning as they made their way to school, but on the return home at lunch time when the eastern sun would be getting to its hottest moment of the day such considerations would have made a huge difference for the young children following the days lessons. In many of the eastern countries, the school day would always begin very early in the morning to ensure that every one could be home at lunchtime before the temperatures of the day had reached their maximum level during the afternoon. It was acknowledged that no one could be expected to give the same measure of concentration as the temperatures soared to its maximum level for the day, and therefore it was better to allow them the opportunity of taking the siesta at home.

A family of six children, through the years, soon tend to accentuate the more personal aspects of stress within the context of an unsettling political environment, and sometimes the combination of the two can bring any family unit dangerously close to the ultimate breaking point as the different factors in life begin to perilously mix together into a poisonous cocktail of emotions. Violet was fully occupied attending to her daily chores, ensuring that all the house work was satisfactorily completed, whilst four year old Jonathan was playing in one corner of the living room. He seemed to be quite happy and contented as he attended to what must always be the most important things, in terms of the priority in the mind of a young four year old boy, the next imaginary game waiting to be played out.

Violet checked that he was alright, sat him down with a cool drink, and reassured him that she was just attending to the bedrooms if he needed her for anything. All he needed to do was call out for help and she would be there for him. She applied herself industriously to her house work, confident that all would be well as she felt fully assured that she would hear of any concerns that he may express, after all, they were all living in the same house so what could possibly go wrong in such an extremely short space of time. The reality, however, is that the events of life will often go wrong at a time when one least expects or desires it to happen. That surprise element will often high light the devastation for those who are living out the consequences of it all, trying to pick up the pieces of shattered dreams and hopes.

Jonathan began to look intently at the four walls that surrounded him, studying them with determination, peering into the corners that lay in each direction, for there was nothing else that he could perceive as deserving his full attention. The walls of the average Royal Air Force married quarters would not normally be seen as being very interesting to anyone. No patterned wall paper, just plain drab distempered walls with absolutely no imagination for colouring, there was nothing there that should prove to be attractive to the average small child, one might think. However, despite that there was a reason for such inquisitiveness by Jonathan on this occasion, hoping that he would catch sight of something that might be living on the walls of the room he was entertaining himself in. There were some new and very interesting experiences here for a young European boy settling into life in the East, as he had recently discovered.

It was not that many evenings previously that he had set his eyes for the first time on the insect eating chitchat lizard. He remembered seeing it as he had peeped through the mosquito net that surrounded his bed each night as his protection from the deadly malaria carrying mosquitoes that were prevalent in the region. The female mosquito was able to feed on human blood and was known for her quick, penetrating bite with its devastating results. Malaria was recognised as being one of the leading causes of disease and death in the world, an infectious disease caused by a parasite that was transmitted by the bite of infected mosquitoes. Common in tropical countries, the disease was characterized by recurring chills and fever, and as such any protection from this potentially fatal disease, such as this net, was crucial.

The fine, see through, mesh construction stopped many insects from biting and disturbing the unsuspecting people using the net as they slept through the hot night, along with the added protection from the prospects of ill health that may come with every bite, although it also restricted the airflow, consequently raising the temperature in a hot tropical climate. With or without the net, they were victims of the environment, but there was no doubt that the better of the two "evils" available to them was to suffer under the heat of the net.

With the added heat, even at night, Jonathan was very easily distracted and drawn to look at other interesting features within the room as his mind would wonder from his imaginary games. He found the Chitchat to be a most fascinating creature, however, that captivated his every attention, and one that he was able to observe in later life in many other eastern countries that he was to visit. Its qualities and characteristics appeared, to him, to be quite unique and came with its own sense of mystery that he could not completely understand. It would sit motionless upon the wall with a tail that was far longer even than its own body, until suddenly it would swiftly reveal from the other direction it also had the most enormous tongue, perhaps even longer than the tail which had already caught his attention, a tongue that would catch and devour any unsuspecting insects that were within reach, of which there were so many in the east. The whole situation was one that he found to be most intriguing.

A lizard living in the house is not exactly a very welcoming thought for many who were arriving in an eastern country for the first time. However, in time they would be able to recognise that this vile looking creature had to be a far better option than the alternative of suffering the many "creepy crawlies" that would certainly abound if it was not for nature's natural remedy, preying on the smaller creatures. This particular creature was an even more inspiring attraction as Jonathan recalled someone seeking to capture a Chitchat later, perhaps feeling that it was not a suitable guest to be residing in the family home.

As the small creature was chased around the room from one wall to another, its assailant was set to gain the considerable shock of finding that all he had was a lizards long tail grasped in his hand, whilst the remainder of his victim, the Chitchat, scurried away into the distance, surviving to enjoy another days hunting of insects and other small unsuspecting creatures. This was a natural defence mechanism that the Chitchat could use whenever it was under attack, of being able to jettison its tail without feeling any personal harm. However, the look of shock and horror seen in the face of its attacker was one that would eternally be unforgettable. The attacker had learnt a valuable lesson that day, chitchats are never easily captured and it's only a fool lacking in a good sense of judgement that would think otherwise. The chitchat was the one who would forever appear to have the upper hand in any conflict, despite the differences in size with the human contesting with him.

As Jonathan looked around, he soon discovered that the object of his attention was not anywhere to be seen on this occasion. He feared that he may never have an opportunity to see this creature again, after it scurried away not completely whole. Of course, he had not yet come to understand that the Chitchat was a nocturnal creature, and would only sit upon the walls of the house after the sun had gone down. Nevertheless, he continued to look around, considering every corner as a possibility for a new sighting. He remembered the lizard as being not too long, no more than about six inches in length. It had very large lidless eyes, and yellow skin. The surface of the middle part of its body, where its stomach or belly would be, was somewhat translucent.

But what was most fascinating for him was to see a creature that possessed abilities which he had no recollection of observing anywhere before. Just to have the ability to stay motionless on the side of a vertical wall was extraordinary in itself, but then to see the swiftness and length of the tongue as it reached for, and easily captured, its prey was beyond belief. He felt a burning desire in his heart to see the creature just one more time. He wanted to discover whether it may have any other unusual abilities for him to observe.

Jonathan remembered the occasion when his mother had seen the most enormous spider, with what appeared to be a huge "balloon" that was seated upon its back. She had never seen such a large spider before. Once again, this was not a welcome sight in the home as she reached for the spray of DDT she knew this was a valuable weapon against such a spider, and would kill instantaneously on touching the spider. However, as she sprayed she was to get the most devastating shock, not realising that the large "balloon" she had seen on its back was where the spider was carrying its young.

As the spider lay there in its final dying moments, it shed the full load that it was carrying; it seemed as if there were now millions of young spiders that were scurrying around in differing directions, instead of just the one she had previously feared on its own. Out of the death of one came life for a multitude. She always regretted taking that one action, realizing with hindsight that it would have been far better, with less to fear, to have suffered the one gigantic spider, than to have had the misfortune of dealing with the millions of smaller ones that would be running in all directions, with all the added concerns that came to mind. At least the larger one was restricted to being only in one place at any given time, whilst the smaller ones appeared to be everywhere at the same time, with little hope of curtailment.

Perhaps one might add the further concern that this would be happening on the veranda, where the Ice Box containing the perishable food for the family would have been stored. It was prior to the days of universal availability of electric Freezers. No such luxuries existed for them. Once a week a man would come and deliver huge blocks of ice which would be placed in the box and perishable food would be placed upon the ice. The ice would be melted by the time of the next delivery, so rather than storing it in the kitchen the ice box would be placed on the veranda where the melted ice would be able to flow out of the hole on the bottom and into the nearby drain. Right near the food storage, and there was the invasion of spiders!

Spiders did not fit very well into the image of the home being a hygienic environment, and being smaller than the mother spider they had the means of being able to fit into smaller spaces and thereby cause greater harm to the environment. Perhaps, on reflection, it would have been far better if Violet had set loose an insect eating creature such as the chitchat rather than using the man made device with all of its deficiencies. Well, thought Jonathan, if we have lost the chitchat that was here performing such a worthwhile job, maybe it's time to find another one, just in case its wonderful abilities were to be needed again. Besides, he decided, it might also prove to become an interesting "pet" for him, even if no one else in the household thought so.

It was at that moment that he made an instantaneous decision without fully appreciating all of the implications that this would have upon others, especially the other members of his family. If there was the possibility of one new experience in the home, how much more must be waiting for him in this locality if he were to take the time to look around? There must be numerous exciting possibilities outside these four walls that were surrounding him, there had to be a whole world of opportunities just waiting for him to discover them. He wanted to explore the possibilities, and to seek out new adventures to interest him, whether it would be the legendary Chitchats, or even some other exotic and strange sights that may be waiting for him to discover. He gingerly tried the door, and it opened with very little effort. He stepped outside into the big wide world, and so began this historic exploratory trip, with little thought crossing his mind of the inevitable consternation he would be leaving in the home behind him.

The sadness that was demonstrated by the lyrics of the song "Heartbreak Hotel", sung by Elvis Presley in the nineteen fifties, would appear to be a triviality in comparison to the thoughts of a family that were concerned about a lost child.Soon after he stepped out of the door, the home would be filled with an immense feeling of alarm, as everyone was mobilised to discover where one young boy may have disappeared to. Between them they tried to think of the most likely places a young boy of his age would have gone to, but not one of them had any idea of what motivated his disappearance. With all the political tension that was being experienced at the time, it did not take much for the imagination of the family to consider all kinds of disturbing possibilities though they continually hoped against hope that their fears would not be realised into unthinkable facts.

With the days temperature in Singapore averaging somewhere between eighty to eighty five degrees Fahrenheit and the nights reaching an average of seventy five degrees Fahrenheit there was little to no need for any heavy clothing to be worn. The thinner the clothing the better was the way for him to go, a pair of sandals and shorts would be all that was necessary whatever may be happening in the course of his expedition. He did not need to think about his need of a coat, he just opened the door and went. The exploratory trip had begun as quickly and as easily as that, with no preparation required.

Much of what had happened that day would inevitably be

lost to the memory as the time went by, for he was still quite young at preschool age, and other experiences would soon cloud over the desire to retain the knowledge of the present experience. He never was to discover another chitchat as he looked around the surrounding neighbourhood; the new pet he hoped for was never to materialize as he walked from one place to another, which was a personal disappointment for him as he searched in vain in every nook and cranny. However, he did discover new sights and experiences that enhanced his personal education in the school of life. It seemed, to him, that he must have walked for miles that day, as he went from street to street. He looked in every possible direction, seeking out the lizards, looking under any stones or crevices that may have been about, but not one of them was to be found hiding anywhere.

Occassionally he would observe the helicopters that were swooping overhead. Helicopters were the most versatile flying machines in existence. This versatility gave the pilot complete access to three dimensional space in a way that no airplane could possibly manage to accomplish. The amazing flexibility of helicopters meant that they possessed that magical ability which ensured that they could fly almost anywhere, enabling them to hover and land in a field, on a boat, a tower block or even a moving lorry. The helicopters had become a common feature of the island life at this time. It was a part of the security arrangements as they hovered above them and then moved on, seeking out any causes of concern, and giving warnings to those who might be seen below or advise them by megaphone of any restrictions that should be adhered to. Jonathan, however, refused to be distracted and just kept on walking; he had more important matters on his agenda and the helicopter flying above did not feature amongst the important things from his childlike perspective. He had a mission to accomplish, and there was nothing that was going to take pre-eminence from his current perceived purpose in life.

As he wandered down the lane, he would have met up with some Malayan workers that were sat on one side, taking their lunch break. They smiled at him and chatted away in the best broken English that they could manage, and Jonathan likewise responded positively to their expressions of friendship. They kindly shared some of their lunch with him, smiling broadly not merely sharing the pleasantries of conversation but in a practical way demonstrating that it is possible to find a bridge that will cross the cultural divides of life.

These were men who came from very poor backgrounds, possessing very little materially, and yet they were extremely generous as they gave from the heart to this young European boy. As in most countries of Southeast Asia, rice is the staple diet, and is served for lunch, dinner and often breakfast as well. The meal they shared included such things as fried dried anchovies cooked in a dry sambal sauce, and garnished with cucumber slices, hardboiled egg and roasted peanuts, and finally packaged in a banana leaf. Then, to round everything of, they shared the most perfectly baked Kek Lapis Indonesia, which is an Indonesian Spiced Layer cake. Every child is known to appreciate the opportunities they discover to try differing cakes that may be on offer, and Jonathan was no exception to the rule when it comes to having a sweet tooth.

As the eating of the food was completed, they showed Jonathan around the various places where they were working, and pointed out some of the interesting features of the landscape. Occasionally they would break into spontaneous laughter as they recalled various humorous incidents that had occurred at some of the places whilst they had been working. Perhaps with a more mature outlook that comes only with knowing the experiences of life, it would have been more advisable for Jonathan not to have spent so much time with strangers he had never met before, but the fears and concerns that would be seen from an adult perspective did not fit into the life of innocent childhood. He was here to enjoy himself, and appreciated the friendly talk with those he innocently trusted and took at face value for a season, even if he could not understand all the things that were important to them.

The time would soon come, however, when he would become bored with everything, despite the good will he was being shown, and so he waved good bye to these new found friends as he continued the adventurous life of a fearless "explorer". He had enjoyed sharing the conversation, and certainly he appreciated the food, but there were more important things that lay ahead. His mission he had set out on earlier that day was yet to be completed, and he was determined that he would not be detracted from the task in hand. "Selamat jalan", his friends shouted out to him as he left, literally meaning "Have a safe journey", but was the Malayan equivalent of saying good bye an appropriate expression as they parted company with friends. However, Jonathan was satisfied just using the English words he knew that related to the circumstances, "Good bye." It was time for him to move on as they parted as the best of friends. For him, there must be other possibilities ahead.

It was in later years to become a distinctive feature of Jonathan's whole approach to life that whenever he moved into a new district he sought to discover where everything was located in the area. This was something that he would see as being essential as he sought to settle into the new locality and become acclimatized. This was particularly important when he was to live a very nomadic life, studying in fourteen different schools and never living anywhere more than three years maximum by the time he was to reach the age of thirty. It is not possible to adequately adapt to the new circumstances unless one is prepared to take time to find out as much as one can about where one is. He would continue in his experience of life as he was clearly beginning.

As he moved on, he was to meet up with some older boys,

playing near a building that was still under construction. What the building was to be, he was not entirely sure, and in all honesty he did not really care what it was neither. It was certainly a large structure that was being built; at least it appeared to be from a small boy's perspective. They seemed to be having great fun together, whilst no one else was around, and from a child like perspective that was all that mattered in life. The whole idea of considering responsibility was a concept that was still waiting for him to grasp. A huge mound of sand was lying on the ground, possibly intended to be the ingredients mixed in with the cement, and again and again they would each take their turn to jump from the first floor above ground with the aim of landing onto the mound of sand that lay below them. For the young people, it was merely a game in which they imagined they were parachutists that would leap out of the aircraft doors into the great unknown. They each resolved that every attempt that they made was to be the greatest leap of them all as they competed with each other to establish which of them managed the best "parachuting" event.

Parachuting has complex skills that can take thousands of jumps for the parachutist to adequately master the task, but in the world of childish imagination the youngsters were certain they knew all the answers to the occupation from a single jump into the mound, but still they would challenge each other to perfect their skills as they expected the improvement they gained to aspire towards perfection. They could sense some of the atmosphere in it all as the dreams began to feel like reality. Blue skies ahead, warm air surrounding them, fifteen thousand feet freefall at over one hundred and twenty miles per hour, this was all theirs. At least it was in their dreams and imaginations where young people would always sense they had to be invincible. They could conquer the world of parachuting with little effort at all, they reasoned. To add to the reality of it all, they made use of umbrellas to create substitute parachutes.

The fictitious Mary Poppins had nothing that could compare with the experiences that were now known to these boys as they flew through the air with umbrellas in hand. As Mary Poppins would have declared, this had to be "supercalifragilisticexialidocious". Umbrellas, made of wood and paper, were in plentiful supply in Singapore, they seemed to be available everywhere that one looked. In a tropical country like Singapore, an umbrella serves to provide shade on a sunny day and keeps you dry on a rainy day. And mind you, it can be bright and sunny and the next moment, it is raining cats and dogs. As the mound of sand was so high, it may not have seemed to be such a great distance for the older boys to jump out, but relatively speaking, it was an unbelievably enormous height for Jonathan and the challenge was one that was real and demanding.

At first he was unsure of whether he should have attempted to join in these adventurous games as he recognised how daunting each leap could be, but it did seem to him that these boys were having some tremendous fun together, and it did fit into his own desire to experience some kind of adventure as he explored the locality. As such, it did not take a lot of encouragement from the boys for him to follow suit, soon becoming oblivious to all the possible risks. So often at a young age it seems that one is like superman, at least within ones imagination, behaving as if one is indestructible, though in reality the risks of life apply to all ages and locations. The initial jump was one that was made with some nervousness, but soon he was running round with enthusiasm like the other boys as he sought out the next jump. He was soon hooked on the adrenaline of the whole experience.

Eventually Jonathan was to tire of all the excitement and returned home, having been away on his adventures for a large part of the day. The door was open and as he entered he wondered if he had been missed by anyone. He soon discovered just how much he was missed as he was met by his distraught family that had been searching everywhere for him in vain. He did not have any comprehension what the fuss could be all about. Why had they been worrying, he knew he was perfectly safe, so what was the concern about? The family was not as sure as they saw him arriving home with cuts and scratches and bruises from his adventures and far from the picture of cleanliness which they knew Jonathan had been when he was last seen in the family home. Where had he been? What had he been doing? Did he not know how dangerous it can be to wander off on his own? Jonathan said not a word; it was to remain a mystery that he was not going to reveal no matter how many times he may have been asked, always to be his secret adventure for the day.

It would not be the only occasion that children would take high risks in life, as many families can testify. The boys were all playing in the ground that lay towards one end of the block of houses where they lived. Along with other children in the neighbourhood, they were playing games in amongst the bamboo trees. Though they were known as bamboo trees, the bamboo was more from the grass family; some of them are known to grow to become giants, growing at a rapid pace by over one metre a day. They would also spread quite quickly through there roots reaching out into new soil and springing up with a new shoot some considerable distance away. In that sense, they could become very invasive as they reached into and established themselves in new territory with little difficulty. They were very versatile and as such have been used in varying cultures of the world in a variety of ways. That versatility therefore would also become a tremendous potential for young boys who were looking for new opportunities to play with different resources. Here were the natural resources they desired for the games they would play, right on their door step without any need for them to search it out. The boys were certain in their own mind that the "adventure playground" was a natural venue for them to enjoy.

As they scrambled around, reaching out to the pliable shoots of the bamboos, there was one young person that was feeling isolated and neglected. Geraldine was far from convinced by the boy's arguments that this was not an appropriate occupation for young girls to be involved in; she wanted to be a part of all the fun and games just the same as them. Maybe she was ahead of her time in this respect, but she believed she had a right to equality irrespective of whether she was male or female. This was the kind of occupation that was only suitable for boys, the boys would claim, but she could not agree with them and was determined to stand her ground as they argued together. They kept trying to encourage her to find something else to do, to find the girls and play more gentle games with them rather than the tough games where girls were definitely meant to be off limits, but nothing would convince her. Towards the front of the housing was a whole expanse of green grass, surely that would be a safer environment for the girls to play in.

Finally, in sheer desperation she brought out what she believed to be the ace card in her arguments. If they would not allow her to join in then she would have no alternative but to let mum know that she was being deliberately excluded from the fun and treated unfairly. She was right; it was her ace card that would radically change the balance of argument. They looked at her, and knew from her look that she was serious. At this point of time the boys were holding down one end of a bamboo tree, which was pliable and had been bent over considerably. In resignation to the inevitable consequences, even if they were unhappy with the prospects, they finally said, alright, if you wish to be involved, grab hold of this bamboo which is bent down whilst we work out what you could possibly do, and do not let go under any circumstances. It is important that you hold it down with all your weight. With a triumphant look of glee, sensing her victory in these delicate negotiations she had been involved in, she agreed to the task and obediently took her place as she was directed.

It was at this point that the neighbour, "Mrs. Jones", who lived in the end terraced house, looked out of her upstairs balcony window in the direction of where the children were playing, screamed in horror, and then collapsed in shock at the terrifying sight that had met her eyes. Flying through the air past her upstairs window, and holding on with grim determination to the bamboo tree exactly as she had been instructed to do, was the young Geraldine! She not only flew through the air, she shot into the sky as if she was a human cannonball fired with all the dangers that go with such an occupation. One of the first human cannonballs was a young teenager, a fourteen year old acrobat girl who went by the stage name of Zazel, otherwise known as Rossa Richter, who made her maiden voyage, so to speak, in April, eighteen seventy seven, but it was to be in the nineteen fifties, however, that Geraldine had this moving experience. She must have had the distinction of not merely being of such ilk at an even earlier age than Rossa was, but also finding herself in such a position without any fore thought of the possibilities that lay before her. Her desire for fun and games had resulted in her reaching heights of excitement never before visualised.

Unfortunately, as some stories are told, during one of the performances carried out by Rossa she broke her back and had to spend the rest of her life in a back brace. Geraldine, however, was far more fortunate in her great adventure in life. How she managed to avoid being injured was to become one of life's great mysteries that were never to be solved in the years that lay before, and yet miraculously she did survive against all the odds. The boys had convincingly proved their point that she was not able to carry out the work of holding the flexible bamboo tree down as well as the boys could, because she did not have the strength of the boys.

However, it was not going to prove so easy for them to convince their dad on his return from work that they did not deserve punishment for allowing their sister to be put into such a risky position. They would be seen as failing in their responsibility, and allowing her to be in such a dangerous position was nothing short of being highly irresponsible. They were in fear and trembling as they waited for the time when father would be arriving home from work, for they knew an unwelcome punishment was bound to be in store for them as the time approached. This was perhaps an early lesson for them that it can be so difficult sometimes to make the correct decisions in life. A decision that had been taken with the hope of avoiding punishment being given to them had, in reality, badly rebounded back on them.

Chapter 3

"Heart break hotel ... or heart transplants?"

Paddy and Violet walked together from street to street, both of them intensely engrossed in their own personal thoughts. The route that they were taking was not their primary concern today, what was far more important to them was their own unique circumstances that needed to be discussed. It was not in any way a romantic stroll; the agenda of this time was a question of how life would proceed for them as a family.

Service life will always bring its own peculiar manifestations of stress in the development of any family, as they each had painfully come to know, and the mental and emotional strain within it can never be left unattended to for too long. There can be so much that can prove to become the means of dividing the greatest and most solid of family units. There would be others that they knew, some who they counted on as being very good friends, who had already experienced what they perceived as being the ultimate cost in the family existence resulting from the stress of service life. Despite the years spent in bonding together the estrangement in families can come so easily if one does not guard against it and become aware of the warning signs that may flash before them at any moment.

As they thought through some of their own personal issues, they knew it was important to talk through everything that may have become a difficult concern for them. There were so many matters for them to address, there would be both the discipline and the social aspects of service life itself, travelling experiences, family life, personal issues, and the whole aspect of what it was that had brought them together, and the means of ensuring that they were to be continuing together. They were aware that such serious and deep conversations were essential for them as a couple, as it would also be imperative for any other couples who may be in the midst of equally difficult circumstances.

The singer, Elvis Pressley was breaking into the top of the pop charts for the first time in nineteen fifty six with his recording of the record "Heart break Hotel", and by the month of April the recording of this song had already hit the number one spot in the United States of America pop charts, selling in excess of a staggering one million recordings. Even in places like Singapore, his voice was beginning to become well known, a familiar sound that would be heard regularly in every home. However, as Elvis Pressley may have sung on this subject, Paddy and Violet knew that heartbreak was the last thing that they wished to experience together. Is there anyone who would consider heart break to be an experience to look forward to with any kind of eagerness? The pain of life's experiences can be so difficult to overcome.

They walked from one area to another; their attention was so preoccupied by these important topics that were concerning their lives that the splendour of the sights which were surrounding them would have been matters that would easily have faded away out of their perspective. Wonderful as these visions may have been, they could not be the focus of attention on this occasion. They soon found themselves in a district that was known as Joo Chiat, which was not very far from the district of Katong where they were living. The distinctive charm of Katong is something that can be traced back to its Peranakan roots. A quiet residential area that was formerly dominated by the wealthy Straits Chinese families or the Peranakans, many of the older Peranakan homes in Katong, which were once seaside villas, were still standing very tall and picturesque.

However, the neighbouring Joo Chiat also had something that was outstanding to be experienced. The whole area was originally a huge coconut plantation which had now been transformed into a bustling enclave and was named after the former plantation owner Chew Joo Chiat, who was a wealthy Peranakan landowner. The Peranakens were the only truly indigenous group to this area, a very old mixture of Chinese and Malays, with their own complex traditions. Since then Joo Chiat has developed and become known as the epitome of Singapore's multiculturalism. There were representatives that could be seen from the Malay, Chinese, Indians, Eurasians and expatriates, and these people would all have lived and shopped peacefully side by side together, as would people who were representative of every possible income group on the island.

Joo Chiat was a district that would be bustling with all kinds of activity both in the daytime as well as in the night. You could find all kinds of shops, restaurants, offices and residential homes all around this area. There was so much that could be seen and experienced in this locality where you could discover traditional spices, herbs, carpets as well as the most beautiful religious artefacts. Shops in this eastern part of Singapore would sell rare Malay and Indonesian spices, Persian carpets and traditional Malay garments such as the baju kurung and baju kebaya. The baju kurung looked quite like what many of the traditional Malayan men would have worn. It was a simple knee length blouse that would be worn over a long skirt that was pleated at the side. The Baju Kebaya was a popular item of clothing amongst the Malayan community. It was a bit like a baju kurung except for the fact that it was much more tightly fitting than the baju kurung would be. There were also plenty of shops to visit that were selling such items as table cloth, curtains and many other household items. Shopping in Joo Chiat was truly a most exhilarating experience.

Then of course, there could be the diversions taken into the market, where shopping was an even more interesting experience and full of various distractions, as one might seek out the purchase of your next chicken for dinner, whilst the unfortunate bird was still alive and able to stare back at you in the face.

Passing the various restaurants, customers would be drawn to the table, attracted by the irresistible temptation of the aromatic waft of slowly simmering creamy coconut curry flavoured with lemon grass and kaffir lime leaves. The wonderful smell of cumin, coriander and cinnamon from the bubbling pot invaded the whole neighbourhood luring everyone to the door. Variety is the spice in Malay food. The traditional culinary style has been greatly influenced by the long ago traders that came from neighbouring countries, such as Indonesia, India, and the Middle East, and also from China. Malay food would often be described as being spicy and flavourful as it would utilize a melting pot of various spices and herbs. For religious reasons, pork is never used in traditional Malay and Indonesian cuisine, both of which were strong Muslim countries, but in other respects there appeared to be very little restrictions as they brought a variety of taste to all that they cooked.

Once inside the restaurant, there was the added temptation of the wide range of desserts that were made available for the customers to purchase. Generally, Malay desserts and cakes are very rich in coconut milk and are great for those who possess a sweet tooth. The dietary temptations were unbelievably impossible to resist.

Yet, on this occasion, none of these things would have caught their attention as they both talked together. The temptations of the locality that lured everyone else in were insufficient to distract this couple from the personal mission they were both engaged in. Indeed, they were so engrossed in their personal conversation that they failed to realise that they were now passing through a part of Singapore which the military authorities had decreed was to be strictly out of bounds to all personnel and their families, and to disobey such a regulation could have had far reaching repercussions. No excuse would have been considered to be acceptable.

When military personnel took their families abroad with them it was on the understanding that the families accepted military law along with the men, with the prospects of a court martial trial if need be rather than a civilian trial. Where they were walking was a place that had become infamous for some of the less savoury parts of life and was notorious for its colourful nightlife in the form of such things as massage parlours and all that would be associated with that kind of activity in the back streets. Certainly, it was not a place any one would deliberately go to if one was concerned with keeping a good reputation. Yet they took notice of nothing that day except for their own concerns that needed to be talked through.

As they talked through the personal aspects of life, they each would have those moments of reflecting back upon their lives that they had each lived up till now. Paddy had been brought up in relatively humble circumstances in a very small terraced house in Nevis Avenue, in the east Belfast suburb of Strandtown, close to the town lands of Ballyhackamore and Bloomfield. The dark looking street stood as a contrast to the brightness of a tropical sunlit street of Singapore. In later years, the nineteen thirty's art decoration of the Strand Cinema on the nearby Holywood

Road was designed to resemble a ship with curved walls and porthole shaped foyer lights, a constant reminder to the roots of the locality in terms of its pre-war focus on ship building, and a reflection of its proximity to the shipyard which was historically seen as a major employer in the locality.

C. S. Lewis, the author of such books as The Chronicles of Narnia, was born and raised in Belfast, but the most important feature of Belfast for Paddy was that this was the place of his roots, and wherever he travelled Belfast would have been the one location he could look back to and remember the family that gave him a start in life. In many respects, however, Singapore and Belfast were worlds apart. They were so completely different in everything that was possible that one could observe.

Paddy was the second of four sons that were born to Charles, a steel worker, and his wife, Tina. Paddy's mother was so convinced that her second child was going to be a girl to complete the set within the family, that she only had one name she would consider calling the expected baby, Thomasina. Yet when baby "Thomasina" finally arrived "she" was most definitely a boy, rather than a girl as was hoped, and the chosen name that was intended to be given no longer seemed to be fitting for the occasion. Yet they had no idea of a boy's name to replace it with. All the parents could think of in the circumstances was to adapt the same name and call him Thompson, which was also the mothers' maiden name, without any middle name for him to opt for later in life. Never was it to be allowed to be abbreviated to such names as Tommy, as far as his mother was concerned, and was most annoyed when she heard a school friend of Thompson referring to him as such. It was ironic that she appeared to have no objection to her own name, Thomasina, being abbreviated to Tina.

However, when he later left home to join the Royal Air Force, Paddy became a natural nickname for this Ulsterman to use to divert from any embarrassment that may have been seen from the feminine origins of his name. There have been other men who have been given feminine sounding names, including some well known examples. The cowboy actor, John Wayne, was given the first name of Marion when he was born, which was vastly different from his stage name along with his tough acting image as a cowboy. Then there was Johnny Cash who sang the song "A boy named Sue" which was understood to be based on a real character known to him that bore a feminine name. However, there is no doubt that no man would willingly desire a feminine name to bear throughout life.

Paddy recalled how he and his three brothers would have shared a bedroom in the attic, whilst his parents would occupy the only other bedroom in the house. Three flights of stairs from the attic was an extremely long way for him to have to go in the middle of the night in the event of an emergency, but worse still was the fact that the toilets he would be seeking were outside in the back yard. On a dark wintry night, that could be quite an experience. Indeed, that would be even more hazardous for him if he should take the wrong door once he had reached the yard, because his father would breed dogs, Jack Russell's.

There was not a lot of space, but there was just enough room for them to be kennelled in the same back yard. Jack Russell's are renowned as possessing plenty of energy that never appears to run out. Throughout the day they expected plenty of exercise and would appreciate plenty of opportunity to run in the country, but at night it was time for them to rest. Dogs do not appreciate being disturbed in the middle of the night, and perhaps even more so, young boys do not appreciate the challenge of being confronted by a distressed dog in the middle of a dark night as they sought to find the toilet facilities.

His parents each held very strong Christian convictions even if they came from different religious perspectives. His father, Charles, was initially a member of the Baptist church before moving his allegiance to the local Brethren assembly, whilst his mother, Thomasina, or Tina as she was known to her friends, was a member of the Methodist church until she later came to the view that it was important that just as the family would spend time together through the week they should also be together on a Sunday and she then brought the whole family together as they worshipped in the Brethren assembly.

She would recall the occasion when she went to her church as usual having bid their farewells to each other, and turned to look over her shoulder and saw her husband, Charles, standing looking back at her. She noticed how lonely he appeared to be looking as he was standing on his own as she went off with the rest of the family. What a sad picture he presented, she thought. In her heart she knew she needed to make that sacrifice for the sake of the whole family and from that day onward the Sundays became one in which they walked to church together. Together, the parents would teach the four boys the importance of a healthy moral quality of living that was appropriate within the context of a Christian family life. Such firm beliefs were central to every aspect of the upbringing of the family as they sought to guide them as they grew in their development into adulthood. They knew there would come a time when the boys would leave the home needing a solid foundation to build the future on.

Though Belfast held the prestige of becoming the capital city of Northern Ireland since the creation of the six counties province of Ulster in nineteen twenty, it still never escaped from the severe unemployment experienced during the depression of the late nineteen twenty's and nineteen thirty's following the Wall street crash in nineteen twenty nine. Those were severely tough times financially for the family, as was the case for so many other families in Belfast. Money was extremely scarce, and families suffered under the difficult budgeting decisions they needed to make, and they each felt to be considerably under threat by the circumstances of life. Joining the British Royal Air Force was seen by most people as an opportunity for

Paddy, or Thompson as the family and neighbours would call him in Belfast, to obtain secure and long term employment. It would also give him the chance to be able to send some financial assistance home that would bring some reassurance to his parents.

However, no matter how true that maybe it was not going to be without some personal cost, and as they bid their farewells Thompson would, like many other young person of any generation discover that the realities of life would never come cheaply, there would be a cost to pay in other respects. It was the nineteen thirty's as he left home. From a political perspective, the dark depressing clouds of war were beginning to hover across much of Europe, clouds that were destined to saturate many families in the pains of life. Here were aspects that would impinge upon the lives of so many people of that era, but as Paddy set off to cross the Irish Sea this was to be the beginning of many personal evaluations that would affect his life in so many ways. Throughout life, there must always be those times when one takes a moment to establish a measured assessment of life, as well as particular situations.

As Paddy walked along the streets of Singapore, he was reminded within his thoughts of how difficult it can be to keep to those family disciplines that had been implanted in his life, whilst also living within a military context. Since joining the Royal Air Force, he had become painfully aware that there were far too many temptations within the world, and isolated from those family roots, and in constant daily close proximity to the peer pressure that surrounded him it seemed so much easier for him to give in to the wishes of others.

Perhaps there were aspects of these temptations that would have made for some of the stress that was being experienced at this time in Singapore. As Paddy and Violet walked along together, they could hear in the distance some singing. The words were new to them, words they had not heard before, yet there still appeared to be something familiar about the singing that came across in a foreign language. He was puzzled by the familiarity of this song. Why should a young Irish Ulsterman from Belfast find some familiarity in the lyrics that were being sung so gustily by these people who were native of Singapore, so far away from his western roots? What could they possibly have in common with each other? The words were Malayan, not English, and went something like this:

Isa, Angka-lah ytangkat,
Osa dan Ksusahan;
Orang tntu dapat berkat
yang minta pada Tuhan,
Brapa susah Kita tanggong?
Brepa berkat pun hilang?
Kerna kita ta'bergantong,
pada isa yang mnang.

As the singing continued in the background, the couple continued to talk about the things that seemed more important to them at this stage. Violet would also have had her thoughts to consider as they walked along. She would have been raised in the south of England, born in a semi-detached house in Kelvin Grove, Sydenham, not too far from the Crystal Palace, in nineteen sixteen. Later the family then moved to Bigginhill in Kent in nineteen twenty nine. Thomas had built a number of houses in the community, and kept two next door to each other, the one which became well known in the locality as "the white house", largely due to its distinctive white colouring. When the new house in Biggin Hill was built, it soon became a fascination for many of the local people, being the first house in the community that included the wonder of modern electricity. Crowds would gather around to see for themselves what could be achieved with this new amazing technology as the lights were officially switched on. Likewise, The White House also developed some fascination with the local people as the house was the first in the community to be connected to the water mains, though a well was still situated in the garden.

By contrast there was the nearby historical Cedar tree planted on the Aperfield estate. There was a popular belief that the cedar tree had been planted after having been brought back from the Crusades in the twelfth Century by Sir Henry de Apuldrefield, the Lord of the Manor, who, with his son Henry, is recorded as having served under Richard the first at Acre in the year eleven ninety one.

Whilst still at Sydenham, she recalled, with some justifiable pride, singing at the Crystal palace as part of a choir from the Sunday school she attended. Crystal Palace had been the place to hear many well known singers at the time, but it was also used at certain times for the local Sunday school choirs to perform.

She was born as one of six girls, though there were also three brothers in the family who all died at quite a young age. The death of the boys would have been the means of much heart break for the parents even if the girls would also bring their own unique contribution of joy to the house hold. There was one older sister, and then came Violet along with her twin sister, Rose. She remembered her father as being a very kindly and patient man who appreciated the cheerful company of the children surrounding him. He was a builder by profession, and when he came home from a hard day's work seemed quite happy to sit down, relax, and allow his daughters to play with his hair as if they were professional hair dressers carrying out their daily routine work. He clearly had a very calm temperament; keeping himself undisturbed by the circumstances that would be surrounding him no matter how much his hair may be pulled and tugged in different directions by the playful girls. Perhaps one aspect the twins were unsure of was when they would be called to his side and referred to as his two "little button holes", as they both were named after flowers, the one called Violet and the other called Rose.

Biggin Hill was a relatively small country community at that time early in the twentieth century, and situated on the top of the North Downs, which is the highest point in the south of England. If a line could have been drawn between Biggin Hill and the Ural Mountains that lay in Russia there would have been nothing that could be found which would be higher in altitude in between. So when the bitterly cold wind would blow across from that easterly direction the local people would expect some extremely severe wintry weather to be experienced on the door step! More severe than the experience of many other parts of England.

Violet was able to recall those times when the community were virtually cut off from the outside world due to huge snow drifts. She would also recall how they would be encouraged to wear the socks that belonged to their father over their boots in the wintry snow, in order to reduce the risk of slipping on the thick ice that surrounded them. On one occasion the roads were so blocked up that the local aerodrome specially opened up its gates and allowed vehicles to take a detour through the airfield, which was less restricted by the snow, and rejoin the main road further along the route. On the other hand, despite the disadvantages of bad weather they knew they benefited from the knowledge that they would never suffer from flooding due to the high altitude of the locality.

This was vastly different from the tropical climate of Singapore, where Violet now lived, but as a young person, she had often dreamed of the possibility of travelling to exotic places such as Asia. Singapore was perhaps the essence of all her youthful ambitions and hopes, in some respects. Eleanor Roosevelt had said, "The future belongs to those who believe in the beauty of their dreams". Violet dreamed, and looked forward to her future.

Violet reflected on the competition she had once won as a child by writing of the dream she had in which she was looking out of the open window to see the branches of tropical trees swaying in the breeze. A dream that was so close to the later experiences she would know of tropical plant life in Singapore. The writing of the poem was also the beginning of a life time's experience of writing poetry that reflected her life and thoughts.

Violet would have been known as being quite an out going adventurous girl as she grew up and, within limits, would have been open to try anything in response to a dare irrespective of how great may have been the risks, and often she would do just that as she entered into the excitement of the activity. She was able to perform the most bizarre antics as a child, yet never be caught due to her unique ability of keeping a straight, and innocent, looking face no matter how guilty she may have really have been. No one believed it could possibly be Violet that was responsible for the misdemeanours.

Violet was the one who would place tacks on the choir seats in the church, and as the choir would sit down, the whole church erupted in laughter as they suddenly jumped up again. All, that is, except for Violet, who looked around with a look of utter amazement, as if to say "who on earth could have done such a terrible thing". Violet was also the spirited young girl who had climbed onto a neighbour's roof, stuffing the chimney with whatever material she could manage to get hold of, and then scrambling down to the ground again as fast as she could. The lady came out soon after, coughing and spluttering from the smoke filled home, gasping for air, as Violet would be seen swinging on the gate, "innocently" asking the neighbour what was wrong and offering her assistance. Likewise within the community of Biggin Hill there was a tree that was fenced off to ensure that young people did not vandalise this important legacy of the past. "The youth of today have no respect" people would say, and on the top of the tree were the initials of one of these young vandals, V.A.H., the one who was known as the innocent Violet Amy Hill.

Has there been much change through the generations? When those of senior years would say "it never would have happened in my day", Violet could never forget that as she grew up in the early twentieth century young people could be just as mischievous as they might be in any subsequent generations that would follow after her. As they say, children will always be children. That's just the way that they have always been. She was the young girl who may not have had much physical height, but certainly had plenty of sparkle in her eye, and determination that there was no challenge that would ever be too great for her. She still had the determination, but as an adult it may not be so easy to keep the sparkle when faced with the responsibilities of life. It is the responsibilities that weigh so heavily on so many people as they advance into the world of adulthood.

As Paddy would recall his own involvement within the Second World War as a Serviceman, so Violet could also recall the part that she had played. She worked for her Father dealing with the administration of the business, as well as acting as his chauffeur whilst he sat in the back seat studying his various plans and designs. However, there was also an expectation that everyone would play their part in the war effort. At the peak of the war, nearly one in six Londoners was involved in some way in civil defence.

The air raid wardens were effectively the front line infantry, with the wide responsibilities and the risks that that suggests. Over eight hundred fire fighters lost their lives and seven thousand were seriously injured. Sometimes repairs had to take place during the actual bombing when a gas main was damaged, for example, repairers had to work while the bombs fell and gas leaked around them. And the following day the instability of collapsed buildings meant rescuers frequently required both skill and also determination and courage as they put their lives at risk. Some actually thrived on the excitement as the adrenaline flowed; others valued having something to do. A sense of solidarity is often quoted as an important factor in coping with it all during such times.

Whilst her father took on the role of organising the local air raid wardens whom he was in charge of, for Violet and her twin sister it was to be taking their place as part of a team working for the London Ambulance service. As they came for the initial interview and the required driving test, all the drivers peeped out of the nearby windows, barely disguising the laughter as they saw the two sisters walking along the street and approach the depot, neither of them being over five feet tall. For them it seemed hilarious that such small young ladies should consider themselves capable of carrying out such an important work. However, the last laugh was destined to be on them when, contrary to expectation, neither the gender nor the height were to be a barrier as both of the sisters were each passed to be more than acceptable to serve their King and country in this way.

In the midst of the bombing, during the London blitz, there was a drastic shortage of ambulances to meet the growing demands of the war. Furniture removal vans had been commandeered, therefore, and adapted and fitted with all that would be necessary for them to function in the new improvised role as ambulances. Being driven by very short ladies would have added to the concerns of some, because it meant that the driver was hard to be seen at the wheel of these large vehicles, as the oncoming drivers experience a feeling of alarm and concerned at the sight of these "driverless" ambulances approaching them.

Night after night they would drive out onto the streets of London, and as the bombing became worse their eyes were opened to the toughness and roughness of everyday life in times of war. The London Blitz, as it was called, was a particularly heavy phase of bombing and took place between the seventh September nineteen forty and the eleventh of May nineteen forty one. During one period of time she recalled that for fifty seven consecutive days, London was bombed either during the day or night. On reaching their target the German bombers dropped hundreds of high explosive and incendiary bombs on the docks and buildings around the dock area as well as other strategic locations. When the raids ended great pillars of smoke could be seen and the sky a bright red caused by the raging fires. The air was filled with a strong sickly smell which gave a clammy feeling of evil in the atmosphere. Fires in fact consumed many portions of the city. The residents sought shelter wherever they could find it, many fleeing to the Underground stations that sheltered as many as one hundred and seventy seven thousand people during the night. In the worst single incident, four hundred and fifty people were killed when a bomb destroyed a school being used as an air raid shelter. Londoners and the world had been introduced to a new weapon of terror and destruction in the arsenal of the twentieth century warfare.

Violet could recall many nights of bombings, but one would stand out particularly in her memory. It was a night when London was ringed and stabbed with fire. The bombers came just after dark, and somehow one could sense from the quick, bitter firing of the guns that there was to be no monkey business this night. Shortly after the sirens wailed every one could hear the Germans grinding overhead. The world could hear the boom, crump, crump, crump, of heavy bombs at their work of tearing buildings apart.

Others would have the privilege of hearing it all from behind closed doors, but not the ambulance drivers as they made their way out on trip after trip. Others would be able to speak of the excitement later of looking from a high building at the London ring of fire and sensing a vast inner excitement that came over all of them, but the ambulance drivers who were in the midst of it all were too concerned for the people in need of rescuing to consider any kind of feelings. They could hear the crackling flames and the yells of firemen. Little fires grew into big ones even as they watched. Big ones died down under the firemen's valour, only to break out again later. The streets were semi-illuminated from the glow. Immediately above the fires the sky was red and angry, and overhead, making a ceiling in the vast heavens, there was a cloud of smoke all in pink. Up in that pink shrouding there were tiny, brilliant specks of flashing light antiaircraft shells bursting. After the flash could be heard the sound. And in the midst of all this lives were expended with such cruelty, a cruelty never to be fully witnessed by those who dropped the bombs of death. About every two minutes a new wave of planes would be over. The motors seemed to grind rather than roar, and to have an angry pulsation, like a bee buzzing in blind fury.

(Violet, in the uniform of the London Ambulance Service)

Violet suddenly came out of her day dreaming reminiscing of youthful exploits. She was startled as she heard the same singing that Paddy had noticed and like him was sure that there was something familiar about what was being sung. The second verse of the singing continued with the words:

Ada—kah pnehoba 'an xai?
Ada—kah ksisahan?
Danltnn putus haran dhulu,
flntn—lth pada ruhan.
Ada—Icah kawrn stia,
Sama sperti TUhafl—JuUh?
Dia tahu angkau a'kvasa:
Iinta dah mnbantu.

There had been so many things that could have distracted them from the conversation as they walked along the road, but the only thing that succeeded was the singing that they both heard in a foreign language, a language they had not so far felt drawn to familiarise themselves with. What could this singing possibly have in common with this Irish man from Belfast and his English wife? What could be the reason for its attraction that was drawing them both in? They could see the house where the singing was coming from, a wooden house with a sign indicating the name of the house, "Peace Cove". Peace? Now that was something that they yearned for in their lives, but it always seemed to be just out of reach within the hustle and bustle of the life styles they had become accustomed to. Could it be possible that the people singing had discovered the secret of peace that they desired so much? A bus stop was situated outside, providing the opportunity for them to stand outside the house listening without appearing to be drawing attention to themselves. They did not wish anyone to think they were intending to do anything inappropriate. The third verse continued as did the first two.

Kalau kita tangong susah,
Dan pnchoha'an dunia,
Isa yang mbri annugrah
Pinha—lah K—Pada-nya,
Hikalau kawan—mu undor,
Hatap—Jah prda Tuhan;
Dia risai dan nghibor,
flia tuntu lindongkan.

Violet still could not understand why, but there was something about the singing that was attracting her. She had this inner compulsion that seemed to be drawing her over to find out more. She needed to find the singers, but what was the power behind the singing that had this affect upon her. As she shared her feelings with Paddy, he was not as sure about the wisdom of what she wanted to do. Desperately he was endeavouring to rationalize their actions. He was realizing just how far they had strayed into forbidden territory. The military had laid out the orders very clearly, and if they were caught they would be in serious trouble. Besides, he thought, he was sure that this was not a safe place to be, there were dangers here that they could not understand.

As they spoke, he also said that he thought that the singers could even be a part of some strange cult. He pleaded with her not to trust her instincts, and to turn round with him and head in the opposite direction as fast as possible. Violet disagreed and was as insistent as Paddy concerning what was the right thing to do. Finally, Paddy spoke strongly and loudly of his disapproval, forbidding her to contemplate such silly and dangerous notions. Knowing Violet as he did, he should have realized that was not a wise approach to have taken. That was sufficient to resurrect her youthful rebellious spirit which had been lying dormant for a while. She rushed in the direction of the singing before she could be stopped, and Paddy followed behind her just as quickly, feeling that he could not leave this wife of his to follow such foolish ideas on her own.

Lim lee Hay was sat in his home enjoying the company of his friends. He and his wife were members of a local Methodist church known as the Geylang Straits Chinese Methodist Church and he was aware that it did not seem that long ago that he had spoken with his minister about his desire to play his part in the Christian work in the neighbourhood. His Minister, Pastor Chew Hock Hin, listened respectfully as they each shared various thoughts on the subject. Lim lee Hay treasured his home and had named it to reflect both the sense of this home being a refuge from the troubles of the world, and also to reflect upon the faith he and his wife knew. "Peace Cove", as they called the house, was a home that displayed a peace that passes all human understanding, but not because of the building in itself, but because it was the home of those seeking to live lives at peace with God and with their fellow men.

This day was to be the start of special home meetings that had arisen out of those initial discussions exchanged between the Pastor and Lim Lee Hay. They were unsure how the meetings would develop, but they had an overall vision that was driving them forward, and that was the hope to use the home as a channel for the local people to discover what Christianity was meant to be. When working with people, rather than machines, it is often beneficial to have a flexible approach in order that one might recognise the uniqueness of each individual and their particular needs and aspirations in life. The failure of people to move away from the rigidity of approach tied into preconceived theories and ideas is so very often the reason for ultimate failure in helping the fellow mankind.

The windows of the house were left wide open allowing for

some means of ventilation for comfort, as would be the normal life style in many of the hot countries in those days, when the luxury of the modern air conditioning facilities had yet to be introduced into society. As such, there could never be any little secrets that may be hidden away to be considered confidential; the whole world knew what was being discussed in the neighbouring houses, every one's life was destined to be like an open book that was waiting to be read by any one and every one, and eventually they would do just that. As people stood idly waiting at the nearby bus stop they would often take the opportunity of listening into conversations that may have initially been intended to be of a private nature.

The friends prayed together concerning what they might do, and expressed their hearts burning desire to be a means of sharing genuine love and concern in its purity to those who were living around them. It was at this point that Lim Lee Hay spoke up and said that whatever programme they may begin he felt this inner sense inside him that they should be singing something, and they should begin now. What should they sing? Lim Lee Hay was a good singer with a very strong powerful voice, and was also an accomplished linguist with a number of languages that he had mastered and could speak fluently, and so he immediately struck up the notes vocally as he began singing something that he knew well in the Malay tongue, one of the languages that he was very skilled in. The words that he sang went something like this:

Isa, Angka-lah ytangkat,
Osa dan Ksusahan;
Orang tntu dapat berkat
yang minta pada Tuhan,
Brapa susah Kita tanggong?
Brepa berkat pun hilang?
Kerna kita ta'bergantong,
pada isa yang mnang.

They all knew the words and the tune well, and joined in the singing almost immediately, bringing a harmonious presentation as they sung together. As the singing continued now with little assistance required from him now that the group had started, Lim Lee Hay allowed himself the privilege of glancing through the open window and observing the two Europeans who were by this time standing at the nearby bus stop. They seemed to be having a deep conversation, and occasionally looking in his direction. There was nothing unusual in anyone standing by a bus stop, after all that's exactly what a bus stop is meant to be for, a place for people to wait until the appropriate bus should come by to take them to their intended destination. However, though he could not hear what they were saying to each other, he sensed that there was more to these two bystanders than just a need to wait for the next scheduled bus. He could see the body language and something of the facial expressions that were being displayed, and that was sufficient information for him to grasp that these were people with deep personal needs that were required to be met, he sensed they needed to talk with someone.

Slowly he stood up and made his way across to the door, and then stood in the open entrance just at the moment when Violet hurriedly arrived at the very same doorway, followed closely by her husband, Paddy. Lim Lee Hay greeted them with a warm and welcoming smile, and then politely asked if he could be of any assistance to the two of them. As was the case with the Malay, likewise he could speak English fluently as well and there were clearly no difficulties in his abilities to communicate with the spoken language across the racial barriers.

Violet thought for a moment, unsure now whether the enquiry she had originally intended to make of him would make any sense after all, and then summoning up all of her inner courage said to him, "I could hear your singing down the road, and it was so wonderful to hear you all singing so well. Can I ask what you were singing? The tune sounded so familiar to us, but we are unsure of what it might be" Lim lee Hay had little need to say anything to them at that point, he merely began singing the same tune as they had been singing before, but on this occasion he was using the English words instead, the natural tongue for Paddy and Violet and therefore a language that all of them present could understand. He was completely unconcerned about the possibility of others who may have been hearing him, and with no indication of embarrassment he continued loudly singing outside in the open doorway.

"What a friend we have in Jesus,
All our sins and grief's to bear
What a privilege to carry,
Everything to God in prayer."

At that moment Paddy and Violet looked at each other knowingly. Of course the tune being sung was very familiar to them; they knew they had both grown up in families where such singing would have been regularly happening within the home. It was a Christian hymn they would also have sung in their respective churches that they had attended in their youth, a hymn that would continue to be well known in Christian communities back in Britain and other parts of the world. The words that were being sung also seemed so appropriate for their own lives at this point. They needed a friend that they could talk to every day, one who was always available to listen to them. Whatever may be going wrong in their lives together, they both knew that the wise way forward for them was to take everything to God in prayer, and then to leave it with Him confident that he could meet their every need. In the midst of trying to resolve life's difficulties they had sadly forgotten the Christian upbringing of their childhood.

Yet they were still unsure of how much of their concerns

that they should be readily admitting to someone who was still very much a perfect stranger to them. Perhaps there was still a certain amount of European pride that needed to be dealt with, a reluctance to admit to the possession of any weaknesses that needed to be eradicated from their lives. Sir Winston Churchill once said "Men stumble over the truth from time to time, but most pick themselves up and hurry off as if nothing happened." They were in danger of becoming a part of the group who hurried off without addressing the truth they had stumbled on that day, lost in the figures of statistics of those who had the opportunity to overcome, but walked on by.

Paddy was still quite anxious to be given some reassurance that these people were genuine and sound. Lim lee Hay appeared to be some one that could be trusted, but there was still some concern that Paddy had in case it should happen that these people were part of some way out cult or strange sect, besides, there had also been all these demonstrations against the British by the Chinese, suppose this was some kind of cunning trap they were being enticed into. His natural suspicious mind would say you can never be too sure on these things, appearances are not necessarily the best guide, and it is always for the best to take time to check everything out. That needed to be a priority for them, he thought. As the old adage goes; it is always better safe than sorry. They may have been singing a wonderful and inspiring Christian hymn, but that could always have been a "smoke screen", he thought. Paddy decided he had no choice in the matter but to be bold and confront him directly as to whom he could have represented.

Lim lee Hay understood those concerns Paddy was expressing as he gave his reply to the query, "First and foremost," he said, "we are Christians with a common concern with every other Christian to present Gods love in the world. That's just how it should be for anyone who professes to be a follower of Christ. However, if you wish to know which denomination we are, then we are called Methodists." That was the last reply that Paddy had expected to be given. With his own mother being a Methodist originally, his guard was down, as they say. There were no other arguments that he could give, and he was now prepared to give these folks a bit more of a chance when it came down to a question of being trusted. Lim Lee Hay explained that they were members of the Geylang Straits Chinese Methodist Church but this was the first occasion that a small number of them had met for this house meeting. Paddy had lots of questions now, and Lim Lee Hay responded by explaining as much as he could.

The church had begun with a vision in the nineteen thirty's to reach out to the Straits born Chinese that were living in the vicinity of Geylang, Joo Chiat, and Katong. They were Peranakan Chinese, an indigenous people of Singapore who were an affluent community that contributed substantially to the social and economic development of Singapore. Their ancestors evolved in Melaka, Penang and Singapore and in the Indian language 'peranakan' means 'speakers of a foreign tongue'. Their Chinese ancestors married or made union with local women; and spoke little or no Chinese. They would, however, speak Baba Malay. They were 'Chinese in spirit and traditions but Malay in form'. So Lim Lee Hay explained that these were people who needed a unique presentation of the same Christian truth. There may be differences in background amongst the multicultural traditions of Singapore, but the centre piece of all that they believed to be essential revolved around a verse of the bible that spoke eloquently of God's love for the world. He began to quote the biblical verse from John's gospel, chapter three, and verse sixteen. He knew the verse perfectly from his memory. "For God so loved the world that he gave his only begotten son that whosoever believed in him might not perish but have everlasting life".

The church confidently believed that God had provided the

right person to lead them back in the nineteen thirty's, Pastor Chew Hock Hin, who gave up his very successful business career in order to answer God's call to serve the church. The first worship service to be conducted in the Peranakan language was held on Pentecost Sunday on the fifteenth of May nineteen thirty three at Geylang Straits Chinese Methodist Church with the Reverend Chew Hock Hin appointed as their founder Pastor. This was the same Pastor who still served the church as they spoke together, and had seen the church flourish from such small beginnings, the Pastor who had more recently guided Lim Lee Hay in this venture of outreach.

During the remainder of the time that the family were to be in Singapore Paddy and Violet were to become very good friends of Lim Lee Hay and visited each other often. On the numerous visits that they were to make to this home, Peace Cove, they were often to be pleasantly surprised as they came to meet a number of very important and influential people in the Singaporean society, largely due to the fact that their host was related to the Chief Minister on the island, Lim Yew Hock, though as is the case in many societies it was soon clear that not all of these influential people would have shared the same strong Christian convictions that were held by Lim Lee Hay.

The Chinese people tended to use the family name first, rather than the European method of putting the family name last. As such, the friends would soon come to refer to Lim Lee Hay with the less formal greeting of Lee Hay, just as he would come to refer to them as Paddy and Violet. Despite all of the important people that Paddy and Violet were to meet and have such deep conversations with during their visits, there was one thing that struck them both, and which would ultimately change their lives completely, that would be the recollection of hearing the quotation that they heard from the mouth of Lee Hay, the biblical quotation that he had been able to recite to them from John's gospel chapter three and verse sixteen. Could it really be possible that God so loved them personally? Could it be that there was really some kind of hope for them? Was that too much for them to hope for?

On that initial meeting at "Peace Cove", it was this particular verse that they both wanted to talk about, but how do two Europeans explain that though the country where they were born has, for centuries, sent missionaries around the world they still had neglected to give their full personal attention to this biblical verse in terms of applying it directly to their own lives? Violet then thought of their own six children back at home as she realized the perfect way of keeping contact with these people without revealing this vital issue that was missing from their spiritual lives.

She explained that they have not been in Singapore very long and wondered if there was a Sunday school for the children. They would love to find somewhere for the children to be sent so that they would have a spiritual guidance in their lives, but had not yet found somewhere that was suitable for them. Things moved very quickly for them after that as Paddy and Violet were not only invited into the home but introduced to a wide number of people that were gathered inside for the meeting that had been taking place. Noticing the warmth of the welcome, as well as the depth and genuineness of the hospitality and friendship that was being shared, Paddy and Violet were sensing an inner glow within themselves. These people really cared about each other as well as themselves.

It was then that Lee Hay made an astute observation, realizing something strange in what he had heard previously. Turning to Paddy and Violet he asked, "Why did you say you wanted to send your children to Sunday school rather than bringing them with you? Your children will not be able to see the value of any Sunday school if mum and dad do not see the value of going with them and sharing some of the learning process. The spiritual journey should be seen as a walk that a family must discover together."

The British Churches, including the ones where Paddy and Violet had been raised, would see the term Sunday school as referring specifically to work that was carried out amongst the children, adults were only there if they happened to have been recruited to be amongst the teaching staff. In Singapore, however, the churches tended to follow the American pattern of Sunday school in terms of having what they called "all age Christian education". They would certainly have the regular Church worship services that Paddy and Violet would be able to recall from their youth. However, in Singapore they also had a Sunday school class for adults as well; the people all explained as they began to speak with great excitement about the classes they were all in and what they had been experiencing in them recently. These people actually looked forward to Sunday, including the Sunday school. They seemed to get so much out of everything that was relating to their church.

Paddy and Violet could not remember when they may have known a church that could affect people so positively as this one appears to have done with them. They wanted to know more, they wanted to be a part of this journey of discovery. They knew that they needed to experience something radical in their lives, and it could just be possible that here was a church that may be able to point them in a new direction for life. As Paddy and Violet made their way home, the conversations that they shared now took on a new twist from when they had begun the walk. The focus of all they had to say now revolved around the events of Peace Cove, and the need of peace in their lives.

They would return, and the topic of that biblical verse would never leave their thoughts. They wanted to know more about the personal application of the love of God in their lives. Yet still they needed to come to that point of admitting that they had a spiritual need in their lives. Would they come to that point of admitting they had a need? Until that time would come into their lives, they sensed that for them there could only be a residence in the "heart break hotel", when God really wanted them to know something better, a spiritual heart transplant. Such a change was the way for a heart full life.

CHAPTER 4

"What will be, will be?"

Whilst these vital spiritual revelations were taking place in the lives of Paddy and Violet, the family continued with their own explorations of life that was lived at its best in Singapore. Raised as a family that travelled so much, they came with a love for adventure and an intense dislike for just keeping within the mundane tourist traps normally frequented by visitors in foreign countries. As one would expect with any typical family, each one of the children came as being unique characters in their own right, their own personalities and personal interests revealed so much of who they were even if they were also part of a wider group known as the family. No doubt, therefore, they would each have a tasting of different aspects of Far Eastern life to take with them into their memories in the years that lay before them. There was certainly a whole variety of interests to capture the attention of any young person that was concerned with the world that surrounded them, with experiences that would be valuable for them to treasure.

David and Kathleen, the twins, may perhaps have remembered the time when they first saw a tiger being carried out of the jungle by men that were dressed in khaki uniforms and carrying rifles. Fierce wild animals such as tigers were not the kind of tales that would be shared by the average student of a school in the west. This kind of thing would never have happened in the United Kingdom, and they were fascinated by this new experience lived out in an eastern tropical existence. It was the kind of experience that brought out the sense of adventure that was always considered to be a living reality of their environment. In the years that followed this vivid image was to continue to be there for them to glean from.

There was also a mystery that surrounded this aspect of the story of the far eastern experiences. Officially all records would indicate that the last wild tiger in Singapore was actually shot dead some years before in nineteen thirty four. Yet there were two of them who saw this event and were able to independently verify the story each of them had given. Kate was later to say as an adult "my recollection is that we were on a bus coming back home from church at Geylang to Changi and going past an area of thick jungle when I saw some men who were dressed in Khaki army clothes carrying a tiger with its legs strapped on a pole. The memory has stayed with me for a long time and at the time thought that I was the only one that saw it, but then discovered David also has similar memories!"

It is possible, however, that this particular tiger had been an escapee from one of the numerous private collections of tigers that could be found on the island. The Singapore zoo itself would have had stringent security arrangements, but it had yet to be established and therefore had no records for that time. The private collections of tigers, however, were an obvious and feasible explanation. There were a large number of such collections in existence at the time which may not have been as secure as the zoo would be.

Dennis also had some interest in the natural environment that surrounded them. He took a keen interest in the world of the butterflies, with there being as many as two hundred and eighty different species of these beautiful and colourful flying insects in Singapore there was always plenty of specimens available. He would begin with the lowly caterpillars that would spend most of their time eating any leaves they could find using their strong mandibles. He would have discovered the caterpillars in the undergrowth and patiently nurtured them through the chrysalis processes until they eventually emerged into the beautiful colourful butterflies as they were destined to be. The emergence of the fully developed adult butterfly was triggered by a variety of factors that would include such matters as the humidity, the temperature, the level of light, and also the time of the day. Most butterflies would be expected to emerge shortly after dawn. As the creature was about to be "reborn" into its new and very much contrasting life compared to the life of a caterpillar, Dennis would be seen standing outside with his arms out stretched. Patiently he was waiting until the new caterpillar began to flutter its wings for the first time, and then to soar to heights that would have seemed to be impossible to the lowly caterpillar.

He appeared to have what some would have called "green fingers". Moving around the locality he was soon to discover that there were opportunities for him to relocate the plants that were growing wild and place them into the family garden. Possibly amongst some of the first plants that he brought to the garden was the banana. The banana plant was a pseudo stem that grew to between six to seven metres tall. Leaves were spirally arranged and could grow to about two point seven metres long and sixty centimetres wide. The banana fruit itself would grow in hanging clusters. There could be up to twenty fruit to a tier, or a hand as they were usually referred to, and up to twenty tiers to a bunch. They were known to be able to spread fairly quickly taking up some considerable space.

Dennis was fully aware of how to harvest the bananas, as well as how to grow them. Harvesting bananas begins with knowing if the bananas are mature enough to harvest. Bananas are generally mature three to six months after flowering. Mature bananas are not harvested when they are yellow; they are harvested while they are still green, but with a slight yellow tint, which is hardly noticeable. The fruit is round and plump instead of a square or sharp angular shape, and does not have any noticeable ribs. Mature bananas are also still hard. The flower bract is dry and breaks off easily from the fruit tip.

However, when you add to them such things as the papaya, as well as other exotic plant life, the garden that Dennis was developing soon took up a characteristic that was completely different from the western counterpart that might have been known by any European family. The Papaya was a large tree like plant, the single stem growing from five to ten metres tall, with spirally arranged leaves that were confined to the top of the trunk; the lower trunk was seen to be conspicuously scarred where leaves and fruit had once been borne. The family had a whole variety of fresh tropical fruit available daily in an era when such possibilities were not freely available in any European home in the west. The scenery contrasted immensely with what may have been seen in the barren rocks of Aden which they had often passed on their sea journeys.

It was at some point during this tour of Singapore that Dennis was discovered to have some kind of unpleasant skin complaint. The legs were in an awful state of what appeared to be a rash that was completely inflamed and sore looking. It was with some considerable concern that Violet took her son to see the doctor, wondering what kind of tropical complaint could have afflicted him. The imagination would have run wild thinking about the range of possibilities that could have been the cause. The doctor shared that concern as he examined him thoroughly with complete professionalism. He was perplexed as to what the answer could be to this conundrum he had stumbled on.

Then, taking another close look at the area of concern he sat up quickly and looked Dennis in the face as he declared he knew exactly what the answer must be. He quizzed him about his differing social activities without getting a lot of response, and then declared it was a simple case that he needed to be disciplined on the dangers of riding bicycles that he was too small for. The result, the Doctor said, was that on this occasion he had been left with the marks where the legs had been rubbing on the bike that was too big for him. The doctor was extremely confident in his diagnosis as he had seen the symptoms displayed in so many young boys before, and therefore was not as worrying as may have been should he have contracted some kind of tropical disease. Dennis, however, never uttered a word in response. Violet took her son out of the door, partly relieved that it was not something more serious and partly embarrassed at wasting the valuable time of the doctor.

As they walked down the road together Dennis began to reciprocate as he made his own diagnosis of the doctor, "He does not know what he is talking about." Taken aback by his comment, Violet enquired as to what he might have meant. "Well," he said, "I have never ridden anyone's bike that was too big for me. The only reason my legs are like this is because of my climbing the coconut trees."

Dennis had never mentioned about the tree climbing before visiting the doctor, this was the first occasion of revealing everything. He had often spent time observing some of the native boys in the locality, apparently, which would have been regularly seen climbing the coconut trees and decided that he could do that just as well as any of them. There would be no branches at the lower level of the tree trunk to assist; it was a case of wrapping ones arms and legs around the tree and then scurrying up as quickly as possible. He had seen the natives with their legs flexed on each side of the tree with the sole of their feet applied around the trunk. They would then place one hand up and behind the tree and the other hand at chest level on the front side of the tree. In that way they applied pressure from both sides lifting them up while also pushing up with their legs by extending them.

Once the coconuts had been cut off and thrown to the ground then it was a matter of doing the same procedure in reverse, though most people would just lower the hands and arms down one at a time whilst allowing the legs and feet to just drag against the tree, which now explains the reason for the visit to the doctors. He was fairly quick in the process of descending, but so was the skin fast in being removed from his fragile legs. There was also the added factor that his tender European skin would not have been so hardened to withstand the dangers as the native boys who had more experience in this realm.

Some people believed that the coconut tree was the symbol of romance in the tropics, but there were also some very practical aspects that may be derived from the tree. Indeed, the coconut has been described by some as being 'one of Nature's greatest gifts to mankind', or even the 'tree of life' because almost every part of the tree could be used in some way to support people in the basics of life. Their leaves were woven, matted, twisted or plaited to make such items as clothing, mats, baskets and roofing; their fruits meanwhile provided food, drink, oil, medicine, containers, fibre for ropes and mats; and then the wood itself helped them to build their houses and boats.

The coconut palm tree could be associated with relaxation and shade, with tall graceful branchless tree trunks growing to be as much as fifty to eighty feet high, and then topped by a crown of light feathery leaves that were as much as fifteen to seventeen feet long. The light grey trunk was ringed at intervals by leaf scars.The coconut fruit had a hard outside shell and white meat beneath with a hollow centre in which there would be clear coconut milk. As such, it was the means of providing people with shelter, food, and drinks. However, for the young boys those wider considerations were not so important, the opportunity of a snack freely available for the picking was inevitably seen as being the greatest motivation of all.

The nearby Village of Changi lay well off the beaten track near to the far eastern tip of the island of Singapore and was seen as being a very sleepy district in contrast to the life that was experienced by those who were living in the busy bustling city. The local beach would have been a magnetic attraction for both the fishermen and the bathers alike, which would be true especially at the weekends when there were no other distractions to be found such as work employment or schooling. It had been reported that there were as many as fifty two different kinds of indigenous primary freshwater fishes that were existing in the waters surrounding Singapore at that time, which had a relatively small coastline.

It was not surprising, therefore, to find that fish was one of the most popular food products in Singapore, and here was the opportunity for the boys to try out their hand at catching the local fish It was true to the fashion that may be recognised with the stories of other fishermen throughout the world, the biggest and most wonderful fish that they had "caught" had mysteriously always managed to escape from the grasp of their captors and got away. In the village itself, there were plenty of bargains that were waiting to be found, such items as t-shirts, carpets, Indian cotton, clothing, shoes, batik dresses, kimonos, which were T-shaped, straight-lined robes that fell to the ankle, and all types of table linen, and all of these items could be purchased at unbelievable bargain prices. Once again, here was another attraction for those who preferred to be shopping.

Then there was the local NAAFI. The initials of NAAFI

stood for Navy, Army Air Force Institutes, and was the official trading organisation for the British forces, created by the Government in nineteen twenty one to run recreational establishments that would be needed by the Armed Forces, and to sell various goods to servicemen and their families. It was during the time of living in Singapore in the nineteen fifties that the NAAFI was to take what at that time would have been seen as being a very radical step of modernisation when it was converted into a supermarket. In the early days of retailing, all products generally were fetched by an assistant from the shelves that were behind the merchant's counter while customers waited patiently in front of the counter and indicated which of the items they wanted to purchase. The supermarket, it seemed, was a self-service store that was offering a wide variety of food and household merchandise and with the added efficiency was able to offer any purchases at a more reasonable price.

This was considered to be big news at the time. No longer was there a need to stand in a queue and wait on the harassed shop staff to get everything of the shelves before paying for the goods. The shop now had everything arranged on shelves in aisles, and the shoppers would work their way along the aisles and help themselves to whatever they needed prior to paying for everything at the till on the way out of the shop. The news soon spread like wild fire, and even the children were excited at the prospects offered to them in the new system. However, the news was to later turn into a source of amusement when they heard about one friend who had innocently thought this was meant to be a literal "helping himself", and wondered why the staff stopped him angrily as he attempted to leave the shop without paying. He genuinely thought that was what was meant by the statement that everyone can "help themselves" to their purchases. When supermarkets were to later become the normal way of life, this may not have been so readily understood. This was a mistake which this young boy would probably never be allowed to forget.

Despite all of these wonderful attractions, it was on one visit into Changi village that the boys were to discover something that was even more alluring to them. As they came into the centre of the village, they saw the biggest crowd imaginable excitedly looking at some strange vehicle parked in the street. This was a new feature in Singaporean life and no one had ever seen the likes of it before, a bubble car! No one could be sure of what it might be. Was it a car? Was it a new form of motor bike? Who knows? But someone had seen that there was a need to invent the bubble car, and here it was openly displayed to the world. Following the Second World War, the motor industry was desperately looking for new ideas for them to attempt in the midst of difficult financial circumstances, and many restrictions that had drastically held them back commercially. This was seen as being an answer to meet the need of the time as they sought to develop the company in a world that had seen too much hope destroyed.

In their short life the bubble cars were soon to become very popular with the young people and also the married man who still yearned for the feel of a motor bike, with all the excitement that went with it, but perhaps his wife was not too keen on the idea of being on the back of one out in the open. There were a number of variations of the bubble car, but this one was known as the BMW Isetta. The Isetta had clearly caused quite a sensation with this introduction to Singaporean life; it was unlike anything they had ever witnessed in Singapore before. It was small, only seven and a half feet long by four and a half feet wide, and was egg shaped, with bubble type windows.

It was a puzzle as to where the occupants may enter and leave the vehicle, as there were no doors in the usual place on the sides. After further investigations were made, gasps of wonder were to be heard as they discovered that the entire front end of the car hinged outwards to allow the occupants entry and in the event of an accident, the driver and passenger could quickly exit through the canvas sunroof. The steering wheel and instrument panel swung out with the single door, as this made access to the single bench seat a lot simpler for them both. The seat provided reasonable comfort for the two occupants, and perhaps also a small child. There were some disadvantages to be discovered with the bubble car. The power came from a two cylinder two stroke motorcycle engine. The Isetta took over thirty seconds to reach thirty miles per hour from rest. The top speed for the car was only about forty five miles per hour.

However, the Isetta was extremely economical and would manage to get somewhere between fifty to seventy miles per gallon of petrol depending on how hard it was driven. The world was desperately short of fuel following the ravages of the war. Whatever the disadvantages, the economical use of fuel was seen to outweigh everything else.

The family had already accepted the concept of interrelating with people that were of different racial or cultural backgrounds. Public expressions of local culture were also something that would also catch the eye of the curious European youngster. The Chinese New Year was such an obvious occasion of seeing many noisy demonstrations with fireworks and firecrackers which were traditionally very popular, and people that were dressed in colourful costumes on the streets celebrating a new historical landmark. Firecrackers were usually strung on a long fused string so it could be left to hang down. Each firecracker was rolled up in red papers, as red was auspicious, with gunpowder in its core. Once it was ignited, the firecracker would then let out a loud popping noise and as they were usually strung together by the hundreds, the firecrackers were known for their deafening explosions that was so loud it was thought to scare away the evil spirits of the past year. The Chinese New Year or Spring Festival was one of the most important traditional Chinese holidays for the Chinese throughout the world. It was sometimes called the Lunar New Year, especially by people outside China including the population of Singapore.

The festival would traditionally begin on the first day of the first lunar month in the Chinese calendar and ended on the fifteenth; this day was called the Lantern Festival. Lanterns would be clearly seen on this occasion. They would be red in colour and tended to be oval in shape. These were the traditional Chinese paper lanterns. The lanterns, used on the fifteenth day of the Chinese New Year for the Lantern Festival, were bright, colourful, and in many different sizes and shapes.So, every January and February, the Lunar New Year was celebrated. It was seen as being the major event in the Chinese calendar. New clothing was usually worn to signify a new year. Dragon dances were common during the Chinese New Year. It was believed that the loud beats of the drum and the deafening sounds of the cymbals together with the face of the dragon dancing aggressively would evict bad or evil spirits.

On the days before the New Year celebration Chinese families would give their home a thorough cleaning. There was a Chinese saying which said "Wash away the dirt on *ninyabaat*". It was believed that the cleaning would sweep away the bad luck that had been known during the preceding year and thereby make their homes ready for good luck that they always hoped for. Brooms and dust pans were then put away on the first day so that luck could not be swept away. Some people gave their homes, doors and window frames a new coat of red paint. Red pieces of paper, which were bearing good wishes in Chinese calligraphy, were pasted on doors and walls.

The main celebration revolved around the reunion dinner on the eve and visits to relatives and friends would then proceed on the first two days. After the reunion dinner had taken place, parents and other relatives distributed what they called 'hong bao', which were red packets containing money, to all the family's unmarried children as a gesture of good fortune. In Singapore, the Chinese New Year was celebrated mainly during the two public holidays. But the celebrations could, however, last for half a month, involving a considerable amount of feasting, festivity and social interaction. Then the fifteenth day was observed as being the close of the festive season. Here was a presentation of a joyful event that could never to be forgotten by any who experienced the event, and in the midst of all that there would be the opportunity of seeing the most awesome float parades that were ever known. As with many other cultures, food was also a part of special celebrations such as the New Year.

Making the dumplings was part of the fun of the occasion, and started with preparing the dough, which was then rolled out into small parcels. The parcels were stuffed with a mixture of minced pork or other kinds of meat, finely chopped vegetables, oil, salt, and water and soya sauce. The dumplings would then be sealed and boiled for a few minutes and eaten with vinegar, hot chilli oil or soya sauce. If one was extremely fond of them, you could make a meal of several dozen of these little parcels, or else combine them with a few other Chinese dishes. The Chinese considered them to be good luck and would often eat them at other times of the year as well. Making the dough may have sounded easy; however, preparing a really good one was very tricky. You needed just the right consistency so that it rolled easily, wasn't too sticky or too dry and didn't break up either while stuffing the dumplings or boiling them. Practice made perfect, of course, as with many things in life, but it certainly took a lot of expertise to make everything just right. Those were counted as being amongst the happy moments of Singapore life, but the sad times would also bring out a new insight from a different culture.

The grief of losing a loved one is one of the hardest things for people to face in life in any culture, and unfortunately it is something which most of us will experience at some point in our time. There were times when the public expression of these moments in Singapore brought out a different perspective upon these occasions. In the traditional Chinese funerals, there would be many decorations presented to represent the expressions of sorrow and also the memories of the deceased. For example, there would be flower wreaths and memorial banners, and they would use a lot of flowers to decorate what they called the repository hall where the service would take place. The burial of the dead was a matter that was taken very seriously in the Chinese society. Improper funeral arrangements can be considered to wreak ill fortune and disaster on the family of the deceased, and was therefore something that had to be avoided.

Within many eastern traditions, respect of the elderly was always seen as being an extremely important aspect to remember. When a person died after reaching the age of eighty, this was a person who was considered to have known a long life. This was a person, therefore, that should be proud of themselves and all that had been achieved in those years. Therefore, the funeral would be arranged differently compared to the procedure involving the death of one who was younger. Usually in an ordinary funeral practice, all the things used in the ceremony would be white, the symbolic colour of mourning amongst the Chinese. It would be customary for any blood relatives and daughters-in-law to wail and cry during mourning as a sign of respect and loyalty to the deceased. The cries would be particularly loud if the deceased had left a large fortune. All the mourners would wear white costumes to express their sorrow.

In a funeral for a person who died after reaching the age of eighty, there would be some red, which was seen as being the colour of good luck, in the decoration. Using both white and red colours in the practice expressed the mixed types of feeling of sorrow and happiness. People would prepare memorial banners that would always be written on white cloth unless the deceased happened to be a person older than eighty when the colour of the cloth would then be red. To represent joyful feelings, people would write memorial banners on red paper instead of white cloth. The coffin was never sealed during the wake. Food would be placed in front of the coffin as an offering to the deceased. The deceased's comb was broken into two, one part would be placed in the coffin and the other would be kept by the family.

The procession to the burial site would then proceed with a considerable amount of noise as gongs were beaten as loudly as possible by the mourners as an attempt to "frighten off the evil spirits." There would be times when the procession would perhaps divert away from what was the intended route in the hope of being able to "confuse any evil spirits that may be attempting to cause them mischief", whilst at the same time throwing money from the procession in the hope that the spirits would become distracted and pick the money up that would have been strewn in different directions. This would certainly have been seen as a dream come true for many young children who quickly discovered that following the funeral procession could become a very profitable exercise for the day as they discovered the money that was intended to keep the evil spirits at bay.

The local people could be very superstitious at the best of times. During the wake there would usually be seen a group of people gambling in the front courtyard of the deceased persons house: it was thought the corpse had to be guarded and gambling helped the guards to stay awake during their vigil; it also was seen as being a means of help to lessen the grief of the participants. After the funeral, all of the clothes that were worn by the mourners were thrown onto a fire and burned to avoid any bad luck associated with death.

The customs around the world are often so very different, and sometimes appear to be so unusual to the strangers who may be visiting the locality. Paddy was never to be allowed to forget the time he attended a wedding wearing a white suit. It was quite common for men in Singapore to wear white suits in the nineteen fifties. However, to wear one at a wedding was perhaps just too much of a reminder of the funeral traditions in the midst of a culture where the colour of white, as opposed to the western use of the colour black, were seen to symbolize mourning. Singapore was well linked with almost all the major countries throughout the world. The Chinese formed to be the majority of the population in Singapore and therefore it would be the Chinese weddings they would have had more contact with, albeit the Christian variations of a Chinese weddings.

Beyond the sights and the customs and traditions, people should always be the most important concern when travelling around the world. Race and colour should never detract from the reality of humanity journeying together. On a previous time of living in Singapore, Jonathan had already learnt that lesson in terms of the care that had been expressed to him. The family, like many others, had the privilege of the services of an amah. This was quite common for many of the British living in the Far East. The amah in the East and South Asia was a woman employed who might be a children's nurse, a domestic servant, or an office cleaner. To take into account the hot weather, many families would employ the amah for a few hours each week to assist with the domestic work, usually employing them through the offices of the British army or Royal Air Force, who had already vetted them for their reliability and trustworthiness, which therefore meant that there was more peace of mind as the employment began.

The native ladies, however, enjoyed the opportunity of spending time with the fair haired European small children. Never neglecting what was intended to be her primary responsibilities; she took the young child under her wing as a voluntary addition to her responsibilities, and would not allow anyone else to assume the art of caring which she had claimed for herself. Often taking him into her own quarters, he was to soon master the Malay language fluently before he could even speak English, his natural language. Sadly, that ability to speak in the Malay was to be forgotten in later life, never to be recaptured. She may not have been like "Mary Poppins" who cared for children in the fictitious tales, flying through the air with her umbrella, but she came with a blend of firmness and care as she assumed her personal responsibility with extreme efficiency.

Coming back to the church, the family was soon to become seen regularly attending the church at Geylang. They developed friedships with many of the families in the church membership. They would always recall the visits and conversations that were shared with the Tan, Tam, and the Kow families. Pictures were kept that recorded the church outings, and the fun that was exchanged at them all, friendships were fostered that were always to be treasured in their hearts.

Perhaps it was a reflection of the cultural background, but it was normal in the church in Singapore for all the ladies to sit on the one side, whilst the men would sit on the other side, whereas in the west churches normally assumed the congregation to be mixed together as they sat in their respective family units. Despite that apparent division the family soon came to sense that there was a delightful oneness of fellowship that they could share in.

As the congregation gathered, a ritual began to develop as they all started to look over their shoulders waiting for two people in particular to walk the full length of the church and take their seats together on the front row. Then would be heard the coos and aahs being expressed as Lim Quah Quee made his way past them all, walking hand in hand with the young European child that he had befriended. Each of them was relaxed in each other's presence. There were so many contrasts that could be seen as they walked down the aisle together. He was Chinese, and the child was European. He was very large for a Chinese gentleman, and the child was very small. He was elderly, and, of course, the child was very young. Yet as they walked together could be discovered the symbolic message that there was nothing that should ever become a barrier to people walking through life together. A celebration of unity is something that must always be considered to be far more desirable in the world than the condemnation of discord.

a birthday party, a celebration in which friends from all directions were united

One Sunday, Lim Quah Quee came to Paddy and Violet with a special request. There was maybe a certain amount of nervousness in his composure, unsure of what the response might be, and yet it was something that was, nevertheless, very important to him, something that he had set his mind on, and as such he knew he desperately needed to summon up the required courage that was needed for him to ask the crucial question that was on his mind. He was anxiously seeking permission from the family to be allowed to "borrow" the young boy, perhaps for a week.

He gave his solemn promise that he would do his best to treat him well, he would be given the very best of everything that he had at his disposal, and he would care for him as if he was his own flesh and blood. He did not need to have such fear as to what the reaction would be; the family had been attending the same church for some considerable time now. They had come to know and to respect Lim Quah Quee very well. They had no doubt in their mind that here was someone that they could not doubt was to be trusted very much, and Jonathan also appeared to be very comfortable in his presence, despite the seeming contrasts the wider world would have envisaged. That was an important part of the considerations before any decisions should be made concerning the child.

(Paddy, with Lim Quah Quee to his left)

The next few days were to become days of great excitement as the suitcase was brought out of storage and the packing was begun for the holiday that lay before Jonathan. Wardrobes and drawers were turned open as everyone sought to help him find the best things that he might take with him. Then they needed to consider the time that lay before. The arrangement was that when they next went to church Lim Quah Quee would take him to his home, and return him on the following week. That wouldn't be that long, the family thought. They would soon be reunited as a family, of course, and then continue with the usual family adventures that they had come to know and love so well. At least, that is what they had thought during all the preparations that were in hand, but surprises are always by nature the things that are made up within the realm of the unexpected. The time ahead was indeed to become made up with surprises that not one of them were ever to have expected to have happened.

The big day had finally arrived. Having bid their farewells, Jonathan set off sat next to Lim Quah Quee in his car, baggage suitably stored in the boot of the vehicle. He had no idea what would be happening in the coming days, except that this was going to be for him such a thrilling experience, like one huge holiday adventure. As soon as they pulled up at the entrance, he knew that he was in for a big treat that was far beyond anything else that he had experienced in his life before. Jonathan looked out of the window to the home they were heading to and his mouth literally opened and his eyes were wide as he looked at what appeared to him to be the nearest he could ever equate to a palace set in Asia. The house he was entering as his new temporary home was far larger than any family home he had ever known before. There was such excitement and energy that filled the air at the home of Lim Quah Quee not just as the car arrived at its destination but throughout the whole time that lay before them.

His host was astute enough to realise that though they both appreciated each other's company, a young child will soon become bored of an adult dominated company, especially if that were to be elderly adults. Every day was to become one that would be filled with young company as he invited many of his younger relatives, as well as the young relatives of those who worked with him. Enthusiasm is always contagious, and so it was on this occasion as the fun spilled over and affected all who came to share in the fun. Each day another company of young people would arrive at the house for another programme of fun, games and laughter. In the midst of the grounds was also a large area that was concreted with a shelter over the top to hide from the sun, a central venue for them all to gather.

Then there were the new experiences of meals. He was to discover there were such a variety of new foods with his guests as he tried the differing Cantonese dishes. He had been offered the European option of food in an attempt to make him feel at home. However, he preferred to eat the same as everyone else. Rice was the staple food in most Chinese cuisine. However, noodles made from several types of flour and cooked in a variety of styles were also popular. The meal would usually consist of rice accompanied by small portions of several types of meat, poultry, fish, and vegetables. The Cantonese dishes he came to appreciate would include Shark's Fin Soup, Crispy Deep Fried Chicken, Spring Rolls, Won Ton Soup, and Roast Suckling Pig. The most delicious of all dishes, however, was perhaps Dim Sum, which consisted of steamed or fried buns, dumplings and pastries stuffed with meat, prawns, sweet sauces or herbs, as well as desserts and fruit. Dim sum literally meant 'touch the heart', and as was indicated already, was a type of Cantonese cuisine, consisting of a wide variety of small dishes, served with Chinese tea, though he was not too keen on the tea itself. The items were usually served in a small steamer basket or on a small plate.

There were important lessons to learn also when it came to eating in a Chinese culture. Jonathan fumbled at first with the utensils laid beside his new friends. They had provided him with the European style of utensils at first, but not wanting to be left out he tried to copy his friends. Initially he laboured under the misperception about chopsticks that both sticks should be moved together in his hand as he picked up a morsel. As his friends gathered round to demonstrate the correct way to him, he found that was only half true. Instead he needed to learn how to be holding one chopstick in place while pivoting the other one to meet it. He looked toward the others as they began to demonstrate to him the best way of using the chopsticks, placing the first chopstick so that the thicker part rested at the base of his thumb and the thinner part rested on the lower side of his middle finger tip. Then he would bring his thumb forward so that it trapped the stick firmly in one place. Then he needed to position the other chopstick so that it was held against the side of his index finger by the end of his thumb. Placing a little pressure on the top chopstick he allowed it to pivot whilst always keeping the bottom chopstick stationary. It took a lot of practice, but eventually it really did appear to be a fairly simple exercise.

In later years this inquisitive spirit would lead him to find out the protocols of eating in different cultures. For example, when in Aden he would find the Arabs were likely to eat with their fingers. Never using the left hand, this was considered to be unhygienic due to the other uses that may be given to that hand. The right hand was the only one to be used when eating with one's fingers or when offering a guest food in Aden. They would genuinely believe they had devised a system that was protective of the hygienic needs, but for Jonathan there would always be a preference for the chopsticks used by the Chinese.

As the days went by, Jonathan soon found that he was feeling well at home with his new environment and was also making new friends all the time. So much so that as the time came for his return home Lim Quah Quee had the unenviable task of explaining that Jonathan was not yet feeling ready to go home. In fact, he explained, he had a good relative who wanted permission to "borrow" him for a couple of days. In reality, it turned out that he was to be "borrowed" by a few more after that ensuring that this adventurous holiday of Jonathan was to now turn into a much extended visit. Lim Quah Quee, however, reassured the parents that he trusted his family well and they were not to worry. In addition, her daughter was training to be a nurse and would know how to care for the child, and it was thought that this would be good nursing experience for her to look after a child for a short time.

For Jonathan's part, however, it was to be a continued aspect of this new education of life as he learnt more about the real Singapore, rather than just the gleanings of a tourist. As he moved around, he found that not everyone had big houses in Singapore; indeed most of them were considerably smaller. The next place he visited, for example, was completely different. It was in a charming and very photogenic fishing village with all the houses built on stilts. It was a different insight into Singaporean life. It was another opportunity of excitement as the family took him out to explore the area, but this time it was by boat as they toured some of the smaller islands that surrounded them setting off with clear blue skies, a warm sun shining in the sky, and in wind speeds of a steady fifteen knots.

Then there was the introduction to this strange thing that adults called romance, even if he did not fully understand what it was all about at the time. The young teenage daughter in the house asked him whether he would like to go out to the cinema as a treat. There was a wonderful film that they could see which she was sure that he would appreciate. He had enjoyed everything else that he had done whilst he was on this holiday so he was quite confident that this was equally going to be enjoyable. However, she said, this was to be an outing that must be kept as their little secret. She had a friend who was coming too, but no one else must be told. It seemed strange, hard for a young boy to understand, but maybe it was to be part of the fun, like a secret agent style game. Whatever the reason, he put it all behind him as he concentrated on this outing to the cinema.

Then as they approached the cinema she saw her friend in the distance, patiently waiting for them. They looked at each other, with a broad smile on each other's face as they recognised the one that was before them. Each of them saw that here was someone special for them and for a fleeting moment forgot that there was a young child beside them. Then in the midst of that magical moment they each turned to the young boy. It clearly was not just a friend as she had said; this was her boyfriend she was meeting. Jonathan could not understand all of what was happening at the time, he just knew that these were two friends who wanted to also be his friend.

They perhaps were nervous of their families knowing of their meeting together, maybe the parents did not approve, and perhaps it was contrary to the cultural expectations of how the male and female relationships should be in that part of the world. How would the world react to their innocent expressions of love? What would they say should they be confronted by anyone? Would they be given any understanding, or would they be severely condemned without a thought of the hurt that would be felt by the young lovers? Jonathan did not know the answers to those kinds of questions, it was beyond his understanding. But he did enjoy the film however, and for a young child that must have been the most important question that needed to be asked. It may be that the child was seen as a means of providing an alibi should they be asked about the events of the day, but no one ever did ask any difficult questions. All that mattered to the wider family was that the young guest had been adequately entertained with the showing of a film. It was the latest film from the Shaw Studios, the Asian equivalent of the American Hollywood, and all of the local population had been talking about the expected release.

It was seemingly destined that this was not to be the only

contact the family would have with the film industry and the two brothers who had made such an influence on the Asian film industry as they established the Shaw studios. Pastor and Mrs Chew Hock Hin were to introduce them to another aspect of this connection, something more than just sitting in a cinema and watching a film. A special conference was to be held, using the facilities of a local school. Chew Hock Hin gave an invitation to Paddy and Violet to see the conference in action. It was an opportunity to see how things were conducted in terms of the national organisation of the Methodist denomination. It was a fascinating experience for them as they went from one part of the conference to another, listening to the various debates that were taking place concerning the ongoing work of the church in Singapore, both within the smaller committee rooms as well as the wider debates being held in the main auditorium.

Then, in the break from the busy schedule, they all sat down for tea with their friends, along with two Chinese gentlemen that were known to the Pastor and his wife, both of whom would have been aged somewhere in their fifties. One of them was short and stubbly; the other was tall and thin. One was clearly more talkative than the other, and strangely enough the one who was quieter appeared more flamboyant in other ways such as his dress and the private interests that were revealed in conversation. And yet the conversation of both of them was still very pleasant. They all talked of the experiences of the day, as well as talking of issues relating to the school building.

It was only later that Paddy and Violet were told that the men that they had just met with were called Run Run Shaw and Run Me Shaw, names which would seem strange to the European, but not so strange to the Asian population. As well as the interest shown in the film industry, they were known to give very large donations to the local schools, including this one which they were spending the day in. Mrs Chew Hock Hin, who was known as Nell to her friends, was someone that worked hard in education and was closely connected with the reorganisation and the development of the Paya Lebar Methodist Girls' School, a Secondary school in Singapore, of which she had been appointed as the Principal. It was within that capacity that she had come to know the two brothers and their generous spirit very well, using the large amount of wealth that was at their disposal to perform good or charitable acts without seeking to make any profit. Therefore, such a meeting with them would not be considered to be out of the normal as they discussed matters of a mutual concern, though it was an interesting insight from Paddy and Violets perspective. Paddy and Violet listened with interest as they heard the story of these two men being recounted. They were aware of the Shaw studios, but did not know much more, and were interested in the stories of the backgrounds of the two brothers.

Shaw was the name that dominated the whole movie business of South East Asia, in particular these two brothers, Run Run Shaw and Run Me Shaw. They were two of six brothers who had originated from mainland China. The China born Shaw Brothers had only one thing in common, it seemed: a desire to make movies and money. Run Me Shaw, short and stubby, handled all the finances of the business affairs, but avoided the limelight. Run Run Shaw, however, was tall and thin. He willfully held conferences at two in the morning, and would buy and sell talent like others may do with cattle. He was definitely the master of the Asian hard sell. Run Me collected race horses, and would name them after the movie paraphernalia, such as Cinemascope, Projector I, Vista Vision II. At his Singapore mansion, he also kept rare orchids and tropical fish, plus four man killing Alsatian hounds that were intended to discourage any thieves that may be on the prowl. Any who may have been foolish enough to attempt to enter the premises illegally were placing themselves in great danger.

The sun rose on the Shaw Brothers in Shanghai in nineteen

twenty three, when Run Run and Run Me, who were down to their last penny, held a sombre parley with two of their other brothers, Run Ji and Run Di. At issue was whether or not they should sell their last remaining family possession, a dilapidated theatre. They decided that they were to sell their house instead and live in the theatre, and then managed to put together a cumbersome stage melodrama called Man from Shensi, which inexplicably became a hit. One reason for the success was that on the first night in which they hoped to open up the prospects of their fortunes, the hero of the show wildly leaped into the air and unexpectedly fell through the rotten floor boards he had hoped to land on. The audience laughed so hard that night that the two brothers made the crash a central part of the play.

When the American silent movies arrived in Shanghai at the beginning of the twentieth century, the brothers bought a movie camera that was called the "foreign devils' magic lens" and helped build up China's huge movie market. Before long, however, the violence and unrest of civil war and revolution wrecked the hopes of the box office. Whenever they opened a movie house in some warlord's domain, Run Run had once recounted, "The warlord's private army would then invade the theatre that was being used without paying, watch the film and then rape any of the women customers."

Stymied in China, the brothers moved into Southeast Asia in nineteen twenty five, their eyes were focused on some four million overseas Chinese. Here was their chance of financial progress being made without being hindered in any way. Run Me went by steerage to Singapore, after the difficulties they had known in China he needed to find the cheapest passenger accommodation that would be on board the ship, which was usually in the area near the rudder and steering gear. As he began his trip he was carrying three of their latest productions in a fibre suitcase. When, on his arrival, he found that no theatres existed to buy his films, he scraped up enough capital to build his own.

This was a fascinating story of how two men had dragged themselves up from a lowly situation to rise to supreme financial heights. It was a story that could easily have been a part of a plot in one of the Shaw Studios films; however this script was drawn from the reality of life. There was no fiction of any kind that would be springing forth from this story of the two brothers' journey from rags to riches. Fascinating as this experience may have been, Paddy and Violet knew that they needed to discover more from life than the issues of a wealthy film industry. They needed to know the stories of real life that would shape their personal experiences that were placed on the path of life before them. What will be the stories that will bed themselves down into their very soul? Only time would tell, though sometimes it can be hard patiently waiting for the passing of time.

CHAPTER 5

"Lay down your arms ....."

In the nineteen fifties there were still a lot of very painful memories surviving from the experiences that were endured during those dark and horrific years of war and the Japanese occupation. Those who had lived through those historic and difficult years in Singapore all had an amazing story to tell, though some would prefer not to speak of the experiences. Some did share their tales, however, and every story that was told was still fresh on their minds as if it were yesterday.

When Paddy and Violet first met up with the members of the Church in Singapore they were a couple completely focused on their own concerns and difficulties. That may be the case for many within human nature, yet there comes a moment when one has to realise that there is something more than ourselves. They were coming to understand that whatever their concerns may have been, and no matter how troublesome their lives may have been, they had never experienced the troubles that were known to the people of Singapore. Even their own difficult war time experiences in the west could never compare with the harrowing circumstances of the Japanese occupation known to the people of Singapore, and yet somehow these people had managed to find a way for them to overcome everything, no matter how distressing it may have been. They had shown their own characters could display the victorious life that could defy the weight of what the world may have put on them during that time, even from the might of the Japanese Imperial army.

They began to recognise that this needed to be a time for them to start to listen to others. Jimi Hendrix was to be quoted as saying in later year's words that were most profound. "Knowledge speaks, but wisdom listens", he said. On one occasion Pastor Chew Hock Hin began to share some of those heart breaking experiences that he had known during the war. Though he was a man of faith as he faced up to his own hardships, he was also a man of compassion for others which was evident as he shared the memories that were still painfully permeated within him from when the Japanese occupation began in Singapore in nineteen forty two on the fifteenth of February. This date was also known to be synonymous with the Chinese New Year in nineteen forty two, but would forever be remembered as being a time that was saturated with the blood of the fallen.

He spoke of how they initially had felt a great sense of relief to find that they had actually survived that initial horrendous day, as they offered thanks in prayer to their Lord for the deliverance that they had been given. Yet the Chinese New Year's Day, normally celebrated with such enthusiasm, was also a strangely quiet day this year, which was a stark contrast to the nerve wrecking noise of the bursting bombs and shells that had been incessantly filling the air all over Singapore earlier. War time can generate such a variety of emotions as one might swing from one experience to another.

In normal peacetime, Singapore would have been known as a happy and colourful city, with houses that were decked with red banners across the doorways, and colourfully dressed children who would be seen darting hither and thither, throwing exploding crackers everywhere and laughing with such free and joyful abandon, completely given over to their emotions of happiness. But this was not normal peace time. Now, there was a mysterious silence that had eerily descended upon the city. It was unnerving, bringing with it an oppressive sense of foreboding. True they were extremely relieved, but without the slightest feelings of joy, what was there to be joyful about? This was the dawn of a new year? This annual event was completely obscured by the immense sense of relief, that the fighting had ceased and the dreaded explosions had stopped, yet also mixed with the concern over such great loss that had been experienced. This was not the time for them to be joyful. This was not the time to celebrate. Surely no one who was in his sane mind would rejoice over the fall of their homeland, Singapore! It took them some time to get used to the bewildering silence that hovered around them. It was as if they had just awakened out of a nightmare, a horrible, crippling fear that everything around them was about to collapse.

Three days after the surrender of Singapore, he spoke of how he had travelled with some friends, giving them a lift in his car, as they went to inspect the condition of their property in Geylang road. What they saw on the way completely sickened them to the core. They saw the devastation of wrecked buildings, dead bodies, some British soldiers with their heads cut off, cars damaged and burnt. Nothing could ever have prepared them for the horrific sights and carnage that had met their eyes on that day. They felt as if their whole world had been completely collapsed in disarray around them.

Singapore was considered by many to be an indispensable part of the British Empire at the time and supposedly it was impregnable as a fortress. The British saw it as being the "Gibraltar in the Far East", but they were soon to be sadly disillusioned with what was then to transpire. The invasion had begun under the cover of darkness during the night of the eighth of February when at least fifty boats that were laden with Japanese soldiers crossed the narrow Johore Straights, which was all that had separated Singapore from the Japanese army on the Malay Peninsula. By morning there were to be many thousands more troops that had landed. The well trained and battle hardened Japanese forces were also supported by the might of aircraft and tanks. The British forces, whose defences had been thinly spread to cover the full length of the island coast line, surrendered unconditionally just seven days following the storming of the island by the enemy. The so called "impregnable fortress" had now fallen. It had in reality been as safe as the "unsinkable Titanic" had been back in nineteen twelve.

The defence plans for Singapore were designed to prevent an attack coming from the sea. The big guns that were placed in Singapore were to be used for firing at large ships. These guns could also be turned landwards to fire at any enemies on the land. However, they were not equipped with the right ammunition to shoot at such enemies. The British could not imagine it to be possible that Singapore could be attacked from the land because the jungles of Johor were very difficult territory for enemy soldiers to move in. They had failed to grasp that the Japanese were well used to jungle warfare. Therefore little was done to defend northern Singapore. The naval base, underground bunkers, big guns and the natural protection of the Johor jungles led the British to believe that Singapore was as strong as a fortress, but they were soon to discover that they were wrong. The "impossible" would soon become the reality of their lives.

With better planning of the defence, along with more accurate intelligence they would have been better concentrated on the side of the Japanese advancement. The British defence against such overwhelming odds could not be sustained any longer. The fall of Singapore to the Japanese Army was considered to be one of the greatest defeats in the history of the

British Army and probably Britain's worst defeat in the Second World War. The British Prime Minister of the time, Winston Churchill, described the fall of Singapore as being "the worst disaster and largest capitulation in British history". The fall of Singapore clearly illustrated the way Japan was going to fight in the Far East with a combination of speed and savagery that only ended with the use of the atomic bomb on Hiroshima in August nineteen forty five.

A few days later, the friends of Chew Hock Hin had hardly settled down to begin normal life when an ammunition dump at Geylang School, half a mile from their house, exploded and thousands of shells and bombs stored there went off in all directions, demolishing houses and killing people in the vicinity. Their house was badly damaged too, but the friends were miraculously preserved from the explosions close by. He also spoke of how all the foreign missionaries were treated as enemy personnel and made to walk sixteen miles from the city to Changi Prison. Some were later taken to the Prisoner of War Camp at Sime Road. There was rigid control of movement and the people's liberties were severely curtailed. For the slightest suspicion, people were arrested as spies or enemies of the state, imprisoned and subjected to cruel torture. Many died in the torture chambers of the Japanese secret police, notoriously known as the Kempeitei.

(Pastor and Mrs Chew Hock Hin)

Food was scarce for them all and the average family did not have more than three days of rice supply a week. Cooking oil was unobtainable, except at exorbitant prices through the black-market. Wheat bread was not available except through the black-market. Palm oil was issued from Government depots, at which, on certain days of the week, long lines of people queued to draw their rations. Similarly, charcoal too was on ration. Meat was a luxury which only the rich could afford.

The Japanese occupation during the war was generally regarded by so many of the Singaporean inhabitants as being the darkest period of the known Singaporean history. The occupation of the island of Singapore by the Japanese was like a very long nightmare that lasted for three and a half long years.

During this period which was known as the Japanese Occupation, the people suffered and lived in constant fear of the Japanese invaders, which was the price that a country always has to pay when it is being occupied by another country.The Japanese had claimed that they were liberating Southeast Asia from the evils of colonialism, but in reality they were considered by the Singaporeans as being far harsher rulers than the British ever were. Each day would bring a new fear into their lives from the Japanese invaders.

In addition to the civilian casualties, numerous atrocities were known to have been committed by the Japanese troops, particularly by the Japanese military's secret police; the Japanese military also used rape and what they would call "comfort women", or women who had been forced into sexual slavery. All women lived in fear of abduction, rape and murder. It was routine to see female corpses that were dumped along roadsides, often horrifically mutilated. All men lived in fear of attracting the notice of Japanese soldiers, who might kill them for a suspected slight or even for no reason at all. Frequently, groups of men were rounded up to be used as living targets for bayonet practice by the troops. Then there was the Sook Ching Massacre of ethnic Chinese, including many civilians who had donated to charities that were intended to aid the war effort in China, and claimed between twenty five thousand and fifty thousand lives in Malaya and Singapore. The Japanese also marched into the British military hospital. There they killed the doctors, hospital staff, patients and even a British Corporal who was lying on the operating table awaiting the surgery that would have enhanced his life.

The people that Paddy and Violet spoke with also referred to the "Chop of Life". This must have been the most treasured item during the Japanese Occupation. Without it, you might have to die. The troops of the Japanese Imperial Army would conduct spot checks. The people had no way of knowing whether they would be given security clearance. If they were cleared, they would get a rectangular mark. If it had been a triangular mark, then they would be taken away and killed. Some had the mark printed on their clothes. The printed area would then be cut and carried around wherever they went. Others had their arms or legs marked. Some people would go for months without bathing for fear that the marks would be washed away.

Living at Changi, the family would often have seen various sites that would have been a reminder of the atrocities that had happened during the war to both Europeans and Asians. During the assault of the Japanese aggression in February nineteen forty two, Changi was targeted as one of the first attacks points, the Japanese army having moved from Puala Ubin to occupy it. It had survived from the dreadful Second World War that took place from nineteen forty two to nineteen forty five, witnessing the brutal tortures towards the prisoners of war that happened there. The RAF base itself was a big reminder in itself. Yet ironically it was also a reminder of the expressions of hope that was also to be seen as if they were small glimpses of light at the end of a very dark tunnel.

The Japanese used the POW's at Changi for forced labour. The formula was very simple – if you worked, you would get food. If you did not work, you would get no food. Men were made to work in the docks where they loaded munitions onto ships. They were also used to clear sewers damaged in the attack on Singapore. The men who were too ill to work relied on those who could work for their food. Sharing what were already meagre supplies became a way of life.

During the Japanese Occupation, the Roberts Barracks Block

one five one at the Changi Military Base was turned into a make shift hospital for the prisoners of war of the Allied Forces. As disease and malnutrition very quickly became rife amongst the captives, the Christian chaplains that were ministering to the sick became particularly influential in maintaining the morale amongst the troops.

One of them, Reverend F.H. Stallard, C.F., obtained permission from a Japanese commander to convert part of the ground floor of the hospital's "Dysentery Wing" into a chapel. It was then dedicated to "Saint Luke the Physician" and became known to everyone thereafter as Saint Luke's Chapel. It was designed by an officer of the eighteenth Division; and the altar rail was also built by the eighteenth Division of Royal Engineers. The font was made and presented to the Chapel by Captain Cook, from the fifth Suffolk Regiment. It was eventually opened on the twelfth of July nineteen forty two for patients, and in particular, for the staff of one nine six, one nine seven and one nine eight Field Ambulances, of the Royal Army Medical Corps Service. They were then to come to celebrate daily with the distribution of Holy Communion.

It was within this setting that the Changi Murals, as they were to be known, were discovered. The Changi Murals were a set of five paintings of a biblical theme that were painted by a man known as Stanley Warren. Stanley was a British bombardier and prisoner of war who were interned at the Changi Prison, during the Japanese Occupation of Singapore in the Second World War. His murals were completed under extremely difficult conditions of sickness, limited materials and hardships. With a message of universal love and forgiveness, they helped to uplift the spirits of the Prisoners of War and the sick when they sought refuge in the prison chapel.

On the thirtieth day of August, nineteen forty two, at the time when Stanley was preparing the draft drawings of the murals, the Japanese began an action which would become known later as the *Selarang Barracks Incident*. It was an incident concerning seventeen thousand Anglo – Australian Prisoners of War who were forced to vacate their buildings and be exposed for nearly five days in the open without water or sanitation for refusing to sign a "No Escape Pledge".

It was against this backdrop that Stanley began to paint the murals. No one had asked the Japanese for permission to draw and at no stage did they interfere with the work he undertook. Considering the purpose of the mural, Stanley felt that the Chapel was basically dedicated to peace and reconciliation, and so he chose universal themes for the murals which would embrace all mankind. Paint was not readily available in the camp, but with the aid of the other prisoners, who unquestionably put themselves at great risk, materials to make the paint were gradually acquired. Brown camouflage paint, a small amount of crimson paint, white oil paint and billiard chalk were found and brought for Stanley to use.

Despite still being very ill Stanley set to work on the murals in early September nineteen forty two. His illness meant that he could only paint for a limited period each day, for perhaps fifteen minutes at a time followed by a rest. To compensate as much as he could for the lack of coloured paint, Stanley resorted to using large brush strokes and big areas of solid colour when painting. In September nineteen forty two, a few weeks after Stanley began painting the murals, he was informed that his work party was to be sent north to Thailand with the purpose of working on the Thai – Burma Railway. A Colonel in charge of the hospital, who knew of his work in progress murals, intervened to have Stanley transferred back to the hospital so that he could continue on his work in the chapel. Most of Stanley's unit who went to the Thai – Burma Railway never returned. Stanley recounted later: "Had I gone with them, most certainly I would have died. So the murals very directly saved my life in the way

I could never have foreseen.... It's a terrible sense of debt ....that one feels to the chapel.

By Christmas nineteen forty two, he had completed his first mural; the *Nativity*. Altogether, Stanley managed to produce five large murals on the walls of the chapel, each mural being about three metres long.

The Chapel furnishings were later moved to Selarang Barracks on the twenty seventh of August nineteen forty three and the areas were closed in. The building and chapel were subsequently used by the Japanese Air Force as a storeroom. The Changi murals were distempered and painted over, with one of the images almost totally destroyed by the Japanese, who blasted the wall to make a doorway. They remained hidden until they were discovered in the late nineteen fifties. The chapel itself was carried and rebuilt in Australia although a copy remained in Changi Prison.

When the Changi Prison was redeveloped, the chapel and museum were relocated outside of the new prison complex. Today, a copy of the chapel and its murals can be found at the Changi Chapel and Museum at 1000, Upper Changi Road North. The original Warren murals, however, are still at the army logistics training centre in the Changi camp.

Though the occupation had a terrible effect upon everyone, Pastor Chew Hock Hin could also speak of how those were years in which his faith was encouraged to grow. There were many examples he could give of how God had intervened quite miraculously in the lives of himself and also the Church members.

It was during the occupation that the gathering for public worship was banned by the Japanese army. For Christians, the desire to gather together in worship and fellowship was always seen as being important. As such, the Pastor and members of the church believed that this was something worth taking a risk for. Each week they would continue to meet and encourage each other. That spirit of encouragement was so important at any time, but even more so in times of hardship. Then, having spent that time together they would proceed with their lives feeling fortified for all the events that may be ahead.

It was on such an occasion as this that their worst fears appeared to materialise. The service was possibly half way through, when the sound of marching soldiers could be heard in the distance. The marching sounds were getting louder as they drew closer, and everyone knew that they were at risk. They had seen the results in others, not merely losing their freedom but in some cases losing their lives in the most horrific of ways. There was a back door exit. Perhaps they could escape that way before the soldiers arrived.

Chew Hock Hin had another suggestion, however. Prayer! They had the courage to meet to worship despite the risks, now is the time to remember the one who they worshipped was more than able to meet all their needs. The congregation looked at each other for a moment, and then agreed to follow the directions of their Pastor as they bowed their heads to pray. Chew Hock Hin lead them in the most emotional prayer that had ever been uttered. None of them knew what would happen to them, but they knew they wanted to stand firm in their loyalty to Christ.

The marching continued to come closer, but they prayed. The marching stopped outside the door, but they continued to pray. The door opened, but still they prayed. One set of feet marched through the door, and the Christians prayed even harder. Chew Hock Hin continued to pray until he felt the prayer had reached its conclusion in terms of addressing his Lord, the Lord who was always the one who he desired to be in control rather than the soldiers. He looked up, opened his eyes, and as he expected it was the Japanese soldiers they had heard marching down the road. What was more of a surprise was to find a smart looking Japanese army officer in front of him, down on his knees.

After a short period of meditation, the officer stood up and began to speak. He explained that he was under orders to bring his soldiers to the building and to disrupt any meeting that he should find taking place. They had expected to have fun, seeing frightened people trying to find a way of escape. Instead, he found a group of people who really believed in their God, so much so that they were prepared to stand their ground and pray with confidence rather than to run away.

The officer explained that when he was in Japan he was raised in a Christian home, but he had left all thoughts of Christianity behind him when he joined the army. Such thoughts did not fit into the life of the Japanese army. He said that as he entered the room that day he was reminded of all that he had left behind, and of how important a life of faith should be. It should have been the end of any future hopes of a Christian meeting that day, but instead the officer gave a solemn promise to Chew Hock Hin and the church members that as long as he was in charge of that area they will never need to fear being disrupted by the soldiers again. They were free to worship. They were free to gather together and enjoy the fellowship they looked forward to. They were at liberty to appreciate that God had answered their prayers.

As Paddy and Violet listened to the story being related by Pastor Chew Hock Hin, they each found it remarkable to see how precious the aspect of Worship was to these Christians in Singapore. Within the West the concept of Church and regular worship did not seem to be taken so seriously. So often it would be for a trivial excuse that the fellowship would be put to one side. For these people, however, they were prepared to put their lives at risk as they gave priority to their worship and fellowship.

They were also struck by how much lives were impacted by prayer. They knew about prayer, but often it could be spoken of without any serious thought as to whether it was something that could be of any "earthly use" to anyone. Prayer was at the heart of this story of Chew Hock Hin, and there was no doubting the sincerity of his belief that it was the communication with God that made the difference, but was this an isolated incident? They stored their thoughts up, in the hope that time would give them an adequate answer.

It was sometime later that another friend appeared at their door. He was seen walking up the road with a chicken following him, attached to a lead that would control the direction the bird would take. Paddy and Violet opened the door to welcome their friend in, but puzzled by his being accompanied by the chicken. The puzzle was soon to have an answer, however, as the chicken was placed in the hands of Paddy. This was a gift for the couple, meat for the meal that lay ahead. Paddy could kill the bird and pluck its feathers before Violet cooked it. It was certainly a generous provision of fresh meat, but Paddy was unsure of his role in the food chain. The friend sensed the discomfort that was being experienced as he offered to take it away, and return another day with bird already prepared for cooking. In the meanwhile, Violet had already got something to offer to the guest.

Paddy was so relieved when the friend returned, this time with the work that he dreaded having already been completed. Much as he appreciated the good will of his friend, he knew he would not have been able to complete the process of killing the bird for himself. Now they were able to talk and relax without worrying about how he might deal with the bird. Talking over a meal is often a good place to be able to relax and to speak openly about subjects that may otherwise be difficult to express. Eventually they spoke of the experiences of Chew Hock Hin and how God had answered prayer in the most amazing way.

Their friend looked at their faces and saw the looks that said, "Could this really be true?" He knew that it was difficult for some to understand, but he also knew what an awesome God it was that he had come to know. He, too, had some miraculous experiences that had touched his life, and so he shared his story with them, whilst Paddy and Violet sat and listened, giving him their undivided attention. The story of Chew Hock Hin may have been amazing, but so was the events they were now about to hear.

They heard of how many of the Chinese were interned by the Japanese soon after the occupation began, particularly those who had connections with main land China. Each morning, it seemed, all the prisoners would be summoned to come out and stand to attention as the Japanese officer marched up and down the rows of worried prisoners. It was not the marching that worried them, but the fear of what would happen once the marching stopped. Each morning they knew that the officer would stop behind the one selected to take his turn to be ceremonially executed, and each morning they asked themselves, "Will it be me?" The death would come with one quick swing of the sword, decapitated, whilst the head would roll into the view of each of the surviving comrades, increasing the sense of horror that each of them would be feeling.

Paddy and Violet looked on as they saw all the emotion welling up inside, thinking of those who had paid the ultimate price it was difficult to speak, but he persevered with his story. He spoke of the day that he was convinced would be his last. He had prayed all the previous night as he resigned himself to whatever the day would bring. As the officer marched along the row behind, one last prayer was expressed, "Lord, you know this is not the manner of death I would choose, nevertheless I place myself in your keeping. Whatever happens I just wish to live and die in a way that brings no disgrace to my faith." He said that at that moment he sensed an unusual feeling of peace.

As the officer stopped behind him he knew that this was that watershed moment that they had all been anticipating. Then something happened which he said he could never explain. As he stood there waiting on his final moment of life, he felt sure he heard a voice. The words were clear and distinct. "There is a hole in the fence straight in front of you. Run! Do not look back, but keep running till you reach the fence and freedom."

So it was that he ran as fast as he could. He had escaped the sword, but would he escape the firing of rifles held by the soldiers? He ran faster than he had ever done before without hesitating or looking back. No one stopped him. No one fired a shot. How could they not see him running? Why did none of the Japanese soldiers fire at him? Not even a warning shot passed in his direction. The fence was getting closer, could it be that the soldiers were playing games with him, waiting until he reached the high fence, a fence that was so high no one could manage to get over it. Could it be that they intended to merely play sport with him, and in front of the fence to finally finish him off?

Then he remembered the rest of the instructions that had mysteriously come to him, "There is a hole in the fence straight in front of you". Whatever the risks maybe, now that the race has begun the fence must continue to be the goal he must aim for. Sure enough, there in front of him was the hole in the fence he was meant to look for as he sought his freedom. He dived through the hole, scurried out of the other side, and claimed his prize of liberty. Paddy and Violet were mesmerised. There was no doubting the sincerity that they could see in the face of their friend; they could not doubt his word. That was two miraculous answers to prayer that Paddy and Violet had now heard of from their friends. It would be stretching the imagination too much to assume that there could be three miracles brought to their attention, or was it?

Violet was out experiencing a "mother and daughter" event with Geraldine. They had been looking forward to this occasion together for some time, but the enjoyment of it all did not seem to be as satisfying as Violet began to become unwell. She was unsure of what was happening to her, but she knew she could not stay out with her daughter as things were if her health should cause difficulties in being able to look after the young girl as she would wish.

Violet was still alert enough to know that she urgently needed to do something as she hailed the first taxi that came past. They stepped inside, and the driver turned to them and asked where they wished to go. Violet looked back at the driver, hearing the words, but for some reason being unable to respond. She looked to her daughter and managed to mouth the word "dad". Paddy, Geraldine's dad, was working at Changi hospital. Fortunately Geraldine understood what her mother was meaning as she instructed the driver to proceed to the hospital.

Violets condition began to deteriorate at a very fast rate as they travelled along. Geraldine looked at her mother as she appeared to go into a very deep sleep. She had, in fact, slipped into a state of unconscious. Geraldine did not understand what was happening, but she was aware her mother was unwell and for some strange reason could not be woken from this sleep that had suddenly come upon her. Arriving at the hospital, the driver expected his fare to be paid, Violet was unable to oblige from her state of unconsciousness, and the young Geraldine was determined that no one should take advantage of her mother. She grabbed hold of her mother's handbag, refusing to allow the driver to retrieve any money to pay the cost of the hire. The angrier the driver became, the tighter she held on to the hand bag. A huge argument developed, which would have been frightening for a young child but would also have been providential as it drew the attention of the medical staff who gathered around realising quickly that there was a desperate medical need to attend to. It must have been extremely frustrating for the driver, but no one considered his payment to be the first priority at this moment.

Violet was indeed very seriously ill having contracted a rare tropical illness. She continued to be in a coma that seemed to never be coming to an end, and which the doctors had no answer to give concerning hope of healing. There was no response to voices, or other sounds, no response to light, no response to pain, or any sort of activity or stimulation going on nearby. She was still alive, but the brain was only functioning at its lowest stage of alertness. Some days went by as the condition continued to grab a hold of Violets apparently "lifeless" body. She just lay there motionless day after day, and it was with a deep measure of concern that Paddy was sent for by the doctor.

He sat there speechless as the doctor addressed him in very serious tones, expressing the medical decision that there was no hope that he could realistically give. The doctor explained that coma survival rates are fifty percent or less, and less than ten percent of people who come out of a coma completely recover from it. Those figures become even more disturbing when the patient is living in the tropics. The length of time that Violet had been in a coma in the tropics is longer means that there is no hope for her medically. He was advised to be prepared for the worst, and consider arrangements for sending the young family back to the United Kingdom. Paddy made his way home attempting to come to terms with the news he had now been given, but he had no idea which way to turn.

Meanwhile, the Minister continued to faithfully make daily pastoral visits, sitting beside Violets bedside as he prayed with extreme fervour. There never seemed to be any response to give him encouragement that he was doing the right thing, but in an exercise of faith he continued to visit regardless. The nursing staff on the ward knew that there was no hope that was considered to be possible for Violet as they sought to merely ensure that she was being kept comfortable as they demonstrated tender loving care to their patient. They did not see much to be gained by someone praying except that it may be a means of bringing comfort to the family. In addition, as the sense of hearing is usually the last sense for a dying person to lose, assuming the hearing was normally good prior to being ill; this could also be seen as a further opportunity to give some spiritual support to the patient. Life may appear to have left the body, but the patient will be hearing the positive words expressed in her presence. It was an integral part of their training that they were to permit spiritual support to be available in accordance with the faith of the patients.

Life appeared to be hopeless, but the day was to eventually come when life would miraculously become hopeful. The patient who was showing no signs of prolonged life began to stir. Hope was returning, albeit a bit at a time. When coming out of a coma, a person will often be confused and can only slowly respond to what's going on. It can take time for the person to start feeling better. So it was for Violet as she made small beginnings in making a recovery that was thought to be impossible just a short while before. As she progressed in regaining her health she started to find there were things emerging in her memory that she never knew should have been there. She started to discuss them with her visitors and the nursing staff. It was on one of those occasions that she spoke of what, for her, was the most vivid memory of all, but a memory that she thought was just a dream. She recalled the "dream" as she envisaged it. She had been laid out in a dark room as she heard a voice. It was a voice of a man praying, and then this same man began reading words that she had heard often before. The words went like this:

The LORD is my shepherd; I shall not be in want.

He makes me lie down in green pastures;
    he leads me beside quiet waters,

He restores my soul.
    He guides me in paths of righteousness
    for his name's sake.

Even though I walk
    through the valley of the shadow of death,
    I will fear no evil,
    for you are with me;
    your rod and your staff,
    they comfort me.

You prepare a table before me
    in the presence of my enemies.
    You anoint my head with oil;
    my cup overflows.

Surely goodness and love will follow me
    all the days of my life,
    and I will dwell in the house of the LORD
    forever."

The nurse looked back at Violet in amazement as she told her of the visit of the Minister who faithfully sat by the hospital bed. The nurse spoke of how everyone had given up on any hope of recovery, except for the Minister. Then the first signs of recovery came as the Minister read from the twenty third psalm, the same psalm that Violet had quoted from. The nurse spoke of her amazement that this happened to be the psalm that was the most vivid of the memories that Violet was able to speak of.

Violet also was struck by what the nurse was saying. Was this the third miracle that Paddy and Violet thought could not be? It was certainly with a touch of irony that on this occasion God chose to bring the answer to prayer closer to home as she was personally in need of Divine help.

CHAPTER 6

"I believe"

It was the winter of late nineteen fifty eight. The family had arrived back in England following the long sea journey into Southampton, and then a train journey to London and ultimately Kent in the South east of England. Violets father, Thomas, had built a retirement home in Jail lane, Bigginhill, in nineteen fifty, where he stayed until his death in nineteen fifty five with his wife, Emily, and his youngest daughter, Winnie. As they settled in with "Gran" and "Aunt Winnie" they would still discover the reminders of Singapore that would emerge for all of them. As we progress though the story some of those reminders will emerge. This was going to be their home for just a few months before ultimately moving on to Warwickshire.

At the bottom of the garden, beyond the tall trees, lay the Royal Air Force airfield. At the front was the narrow lane leading past the old Jail, where long ago the prisoners that were taken from London to Maidstone Jail were accommodated overnight, and then the lane led ultimately to the community of Downe, with its carefully tended gardens, neat cottages and also the home of Charles Darwin at Down House. Downe was a very scattered village, with its weather boarded cottages and the brick and flint houses that were dotted around in all directions but especially to the south.

However, the garden in Jail lane was equally nice, with fruit trees that had evolved into a mini orchard, as well as flowers and vegetation that were well cared for. Aunt Winnie had developed a special interest in the young people in the locality and her warm personality clearly drew these young people to her. When she taught the younger children in the local Sunday school it was noteworthy that the class was to have its highest attendance of keen and interested children looking forward to the next time of meeting up compared to any other time that could be recalled in living history. When she was the leader of the Girl Guides Company, she would often bring a number of her "young ladies" home to try out some of their guiding expertise of camping and camp fire cooking in the garden.

Each morning Winnie would bring the car out of the garage to do the "school run" on her way to work. On a cold wintry day one of the children would need to crank the engine up with the starter handle at the front as was the form for cars of that era, but the car was nevertheless sure to arrive on time. The Primary school that Jonathan began to attend lay back a bit from the Main road in Bigginhill. Jonathan recalled taking a walk down an alleyway that lay between the Baptist Church and Abbots the bakers where Winnie worked on the administration.

Arriving in England, even if it was the place of his birth, was like arriving in a new country and culture for Jonathan. Everything appeared to be so alien to him. There was such a lot to learn, so much for him to make adjustments to, and the realisation that he was learning things that would be considered so basic in this country he had arrived in that his peers would naturally assume everyone ought to know already. There was the humiliation of not understanding what the other boys would mean when they referred to such basic British terminology as a "tanner", or a "bob", or even "half a crown" as they checked their money as they called into a local shop. Deep down, however, Jonathan would laugh to himself as he wondered what reaction he might get if he asked his friends if they knew anything about "Banana money". They had plenty stored in the house, given to them by someone they knew in Singapore.

In Singapore, many British families would have employed a lady known as an Amah as a domestic servant and as THIS family looked back they were aware of good friendships that developed with their Amah. The family recalled the time when the Amah arrived with the large bundle of notes. There were so many notes gathered in the bundle that one could easily be lulled into a false sense of security, feeling as if one had become a very wealthy millionaire with this gift. This was money that was used during the Japanese Occupation in the nineteen forties. By the time the war ended, the "banana money" had no real value and therefore became completely useless in terms of usage for any daily purchases. The Japanese had wanted to curb any anti-Japanese activities, as well as to punish the Chinese who had previously provided aid to the Chinese activists in the Sino-Japanese conflict.

On the twenty second of March nineteen forty two, following the occupation, the Chinese leaders from Malaya and Singapore were penalised and asked to pay a sum of fifty million Straits dollars as "tributary money." As most had already had their property and assets destroyed during the war, it was a monumental task for them to raise this money. In desperation, they finally took a loan of twenty one and a half million dollars from Yokohama Specie Bank at six per cent interest. The incident curtailed the circulation and caused a shortage in the Straits currency.

Banana money

A large quantity of Japanese currency, also known as "banana money", was issued. The exact amount was unknown even to the Japanese, as the currency did not bear any serial number; only block letters. This was the money that the Amah had collected together and presented to the family as a parting gift.

The family settled into the local Baptist Church in Bigginhill where Violets family was already worshipping. There would be many memories surrounding her that Violet would have of her younger days, but now attending church would come with a different insight. The experiences of Singapore had given a fresh spiritual impetus. They all remembered the Pastor of the Methodist church they had attended in Singapore and the various stories he was able to recount of his experiences. Rev Chew had spoken of how he had received Christ into his life as a young teenaged man, endured family persecution and was even thrown out of the house by his father once, but simply would not give up Christ, despite the anguish he had known with those kinds of experiences.

As a young boy Chew Hock Hin was told that he was destined to become a Buddhist priest. It was a matter of pride for the family that they could speak of a relative who could be able to look forward to such a respected future. Maybe it was for that reason that his family were particularly concerned that he should not veer away from the faith that his family held on to. Each day, especially on Festival days, he would be scheduled to make his way down to the local temple and carry out his various religious responsibilities and rites and then walk home again. He knew that his parents had given him strict instructions that he should never go near a Christian church, and he was so keen to be obedient to his family that he would even cross the road and walk on the other side as soon as he was aware that a church was nearby.

One day, as he walked home, something different happened. It was something he found difficult to understand or explain at the time. He could see the Christian church just ahead of him, and prepared to cross the road before he came too close to it. This time, however, there appeared to be an inner compulsion to continue on the same side of the road. This was so out of Character for Hock Hin, this would be the first time he had ventured so close to a building that represented everything his parents had told him to avoid. Respect for the elders is an integral part of eastern culture. He knew that he ought to be obedient to them, they were his parents, but he could not resist this compulsion to keep walking towards the church.

As he reached the church he could hear singing coming from within the building. He was curious. He had never been in a building like that. What is it that happens in there? What is it that is so different from his own religious experiences? What do they do in there that should lead his parents to make such a strong stance forbidding his making any contact with them? Could it really be so bad? This was the first time that he had questioned what his parents would say. How could he doubt their word? In his eastern culture this was something that should never happen. The word of his elders must always be respected. He paused for a moment, debating in his own mind how he could draw together the contradictions between this inner compulsion and the family discipline that had always been so central in his life until this moment.

However, the pause was only for a moment as he then made up his mind with determination to slip into the building to see for himself. As he passed through the door he quickly became aware that there was so much surrounding him that seemed to be so alien. The Buddhist Temples he was familiar with were all very beautiful. There would be a lot of gold in the Temples with amazing statues of Buddha inside for them to focus their worshipping. The worshippers would bring gifts of flowers, food, incense and money and place these as a sacrifice. In all aspects of worship in the Temple, the devotee would be deliberately seeking to create and maintain an attitude of humility.

Any formal service would consist of a lot of chanting of traditional Buddhist beliefs and scriptures, whilst all the time contemplating the Buddha and focusing one's faith completely on him. The worshippers would sit on the floor barefoot facing an image of Buddha and chanting. It was very important that their feet should face away from the image of Buddha. Anything else would be seen as a sign of disrespect to Buddha. Hock Hin looked around the Christian church he had now entered. This was different. In contrast to what he was used to, the building seemed to be so plain and ordinary. There were no idols or replicas of the Christian Deity, no displays of gold, no food for him to find when all the worshippers had gone, and no incense, nothing related to what he was used to.

The singing, the words that were being said, this was all very new to him. He was unsure of everything, and yet these people certainly had a joy and a peace in their lives that they displayed so freely. He had hoped that he could have slipped out as easily as he had entered, but before he managed to leave, one of the leaders spoke with him. Still he could not understand what he was experiencing, but he accepted a gift of a book, what the Christians called a New Testament, the second part of the Bible. He remembered how the Christian leader spoke of a relationship of love that is possible with God, and how the Christian scriptures said that God loved the world he created and desired people to respond to His love. This was different. Buddhism was not centred on the relationship between humanity and God, so this was another new concept for him to grasp.

He slipped the New Testament discreetly into his pocket as he secretly crept into the house and into his room; he was not yet ready to reveal the events of the day to the family. He needed time to evaluate everything, and to ascertain what his inner thoughts were all about. No one was around as he opened up the book and began to read, but the words made no sense to him. It was just a list of names. He read the words again to see if he could make more sense out of it. "The book of the generation of Jesus Christ, the son of David, the son of Abraham. Abraham begat Isaac; and Isaac begat Jacob; and Jacob begat Judas and his brethren." So it continued in this vein, the list of who it was that begat who. He had heard of this Jesus Christ at the church, but who are these other people and how does this genealogy of the past fit into the lives of these twentieth century Christians? He could not make sense of the whole chapter, yet at the same time he felt that he needed to persevere reading further. He felt sure that there must be something hidden within this book that would give some further explanation about these people he had now come to know.

No matter how deep the answer may be buried, he was determined to dig it out. Each night he followed the same routine, as he went to his room to read a bit more. Then, on the following Sunday he went back to the same Church, anxious to learn some more. He was intrigued by all this new information that came his way. During the next few weeks this was the routine that he pursued, until one Sunday he arrived home to be met by his father. His father looked at him sternly; he had heard things from his neighbours that had upset him, and was determined to confront his son with what he had been told. "Hock Hin, I hear that you have been going to the Christian Church. You know that you are forbidden to go there. This is the last warning I will be giving you, remember that no son of mine will continue to attend such a place as that." Then, having issued his warning the father proceeded to beat his teenage son as hard as he could manage, determined that a lesson would be learnt.

Hock Hin went to bed that night feeling very sore. Through the week he would think long and hard about what his father had said. Every bruise he saw, every pain he felt, came as an inevitable reminder of how serious his father was concerning the Christian Church. He pondered in his mind how he could appropriately respond. He felt as if he had been physically destroyed and his life was as good as over, he also knew that he had been raised in an environment where the elders must always be obeyed, so how could he do any different this time? He opened up his New Testament and began to read, he had now reached a part of the New Testament that is known as Johns gospel.

The words seemed to stand out boldly for him on this day. "For God so loved the world (if it includes the world that must include him he thought) that he gave his only begotten son that whoever believes in Him would not perish but have everlasting life." (John 3 verse 16) Those words seemed so clear as it spoke of a God who loved him, here was one who he could also look to who was even more senior than his earthly father, yet one who wanted to find a way to get rid of his burden, not increase it. He now knew there was an answer to all of those questions that were circulating in his mind. In the midst of his feelings of desolation, there was a clear message reaching to the depth of his heart that there is hope. He determined at this moment that he wanted to trust his life to the God of the Christians. He still had a lot to learn, but he had experienced sufficient to know that here was one that he was prepared to trust whole heartedly. The teenage years are often the times when so many decisions are made that affect the life ahead both positively and negatively, but Hock Hin sensed that this was one of his most crucial decisions of life.

On Sunday, he started out on what had now become his routine visit to the Church. He knew the risks that were involved in a visit that many westerners take for granted, but it had now become so important to him, as important as eating his daily food. On this particular visit, he soaked everything in from the service; he was thirsting for every drop of teaching and hungering for every morsel of fellowship that he could gain. He knew that when the time came for his return home, this could become his last opportunity to experience this life with such ease. And as he returned home, he saw the signs were visible as he saw the family home from the distance. There, at the door, was his family, but not just his parents and his siblings. The whole extended family including his cousins was there.

Something major was about to transpire, but what was it to be? Once again, his father looked at him with that same stern expression that was there before as he asked, "Hock Hin, is it true that you have continued to visit the Christian Church?

And do you recall what I said before that no son of mine will continue to attend such a place as that." Hock Hin confirmed that it was true, and that he recalled the previous conversation. How could he forget such a traumatic situation with his parents? Then he heard the words that any young teenager would dread. "Hock Hin, today you have a choice, give up your persistence in attending this Church, and stay within the family, or pick up your bags and leave as one who is no longer a part of this family. If the Church is so important to you then you will be disowned by the family."

How could he answer such an ultimatum? This was still the family that he loved. Hock Hin looked at each member to his extended family before giving his reply. "I love you dad, I love you mum, I love each one of you, and I would give everything I could for all of you, but I cannot deny that Jesus Christ is my Saviour and my Lord. I do not know how I will survive if I have to leave this home, but I trust my Saviour explicitly." With those words expressed, his father handed him his case, already packed, and banished him from his home. It was a tearful farewell, but Hock Hin knew his father meant what he said. The choice he made that day, as he truly did love his family, and he wished that he did not have to face that kind of ultimatum. However, the irony is that as Chew Hock Hin approached the end of his working life he saw the final member of his family following him into a decision to become a Christian.

Perhaps it was partly with that experience of the past that he developed a deep understanding of others experiencing the trauma of life and in need of a compassionate response. It is amazing to see how difficult issues can either destroy, or develop a stronger character. He was truly a shepherd at heart; a pastor who visited his community at home to share his faith with them, and who knew his congregation by name. Rev Chew Hock Hin knew all the children of the families who worshipped at the church, followed them through their school years, and even tracked the careers of his congregation.

* * *

There is another reminder from the times in the Far East that could often be seen having returned to England, the autograph book that Violet had tucked away amongst her possessions. Looking through the pages would be the names of those who she shared on the voyage of life with the family. Along with the names came the words and messages that revealed something of the character and personality of these friends upon the way.

Along with the Chinese names of the people of Singapore, there were also the names of two Europeans. They were the names of two people from the Empire Fowey, the ship they travelled back from Singapore on. There was the First Mate, and also the Captain of the ship, Captain Hill. These were two people who used their influence to support the desire to have a room made available for any who wished to meet for fellowship and worship. For Violet and Paddy, the Christian influences of the past years in Singapore could not be left on the island, it must live on in the voyage of life, or it was all in vain. The room, however, may have been a place to gather, but symbolically it also spoke of something deeper, the personal commitment that came as a result of the hearing of a hymn sung in another language. It was the result of hearing the singing of "What a friend we have in Jesus", sung in Malay, that resulted in one European making a commitment to trust Jesus as her Saviour, and her husband to recommit his life to Jesus, having once left such a commitment behind in his native Ulster. Never could they forget that God so loved THEM that he gave his only begotten son for THEM. A story for the world, yet a story that was personal for them.

They came to understand that history is HIS story, the story of how Gods grace and love has made the difference to the world through the ages, even for them personally. And so, from the paradise island, Singapore, two Europeans began their own spiritual "heavenly journey", understanding God had a plan for them that is intended to last eternally.

The Heroine begins a new chapter.

It was December 2009 that was to see the beginning of the next chapter in the life of Violet, and a chapter that was to last an eternity. Other characters had already gone before. Paddy was to retire from the Royal Air Force at the age of fifty five in nineteen seventy two and settle in Bradford, West Yorkshire, England. Sadly, he was to die from Cancer in December nineteen seventy seven. Violets sister, Winnie, was to die in tragic circumstances in 2005 as a result of being mugged by a man in Bigginhill.

Violet was to persevere a relatively active life despite health issues one would naturally expect from one in her nineties. She was still reading widely and completing her crossword puzzles. She was a lady with a strong faith who was confident of the eternal promises that lay ahead. They say that old soldiers never die, they just fade away, but in like manner heroines never die, they just begin a new chapter.

Violet was the heroine of "From barren rocks to living stones" as well as this book now being read. Many who read the previous book have spoken of how much they were struck by the fact that she was the one who was crucial in the difficult moments of life. Whether it was the times of sheltering from bombings, living with the experiences of being subject to gunfire, or preparing a family for an evacuation out of the country with half an hour's notice of gathering essentials, she was the one who made the difference. Her cool and calm exterior was sufficient to bring reassurance to those of us who were accompanying her.

Following on from the stories of this book, as well as "From barren rocks to living stones", there is clearly a wealth of material waiting to be published as the heroine made her way through the journey of life. But this last month of life had shown that there was more to come as she sought to reassure those left behind. She had no fear of the death that lay ahead. She had a strong faith and was confident that this was not the end, but the beginning of a new chapter of life, even if the process of dying was a rough, tough journey. In the space of one month saw a dramatic change, initially with a fall the full length of the stairs of her home in the midst of the night, followed by a stroke, a leaking heart valve, and finally pneumonia. Despite the difficulties of being able to communicate due to the stroke, she was still able to quote from the twenty third psalm as she encouraged and comforted those who would be left behind. The heroine lives on, but the gratitude for the cool lady who shaped lives of so many others will forever be expressed.

A Chinese proverb states, "The journey of a thousand miles once began with a single step." The eternal journey of life begins also with one step, a step of faith. More than just the Paradise island, the heavenly journey is complete for her.

Printed in Great Britain
by Amazon.co.uk, Ltd.,
Marston Gate.